SEX GAMES IN HOLLYWOOD

And Around the World

by

Michael Selsman

Sex in Hollywood Copyright © 2018 by Michael Selsman   All rights reserved. Printed in the United States of America and in the United Kingdom.

Except as permitted by the United States Copyright Act of 1976, no part of this publication may be reproduced, stored in a retrieval system or transmitted, in any form or by any means, electronic, mechanical, photocopying, recording, or otherwise without the prior written permission of the publisher.

ISBN-13: 978-1-64136-155-2
ISBN-10: 1-64136-155-7

Visit us at www.troikapublishinggroup.com

SEX GAMES IN HOLLYWOOD
And Around the World

'The ladder of success in Hollywood is usually a press agent, actor, director, producer, leading man; and you are a star if you sleep with each of them in that order. Crude, but true'. **Hedy Lamarr**

It didn't end with Harvey Weinstein, who was just arrested – and it didn't begin with him, either. In fact, it's been there since the beginning of the movie industry, and it's happening right now. Harvey got what was coming to him – and it almost seems like he was begging for it. He was fat, gross, and his breath stank from his cigars. He was the ugliest kid in high school and he couldn't have gotten laid in a woman's prison with a fistful of pardons. And he was overt – probably his biggest error.

Hollywood history is replete with sex perversion – Donald Trump, Bill Cosby, Morgan Freeman, whose comment was, "80 years, down the drain," Roman Polanski, Brett Ratner, Mario Batali, whose 5 restaurants closed in Las Vegas, and elsewhere, Ben Vereen, Russell Simmons, Steven Seagal, Paul Haggis, Michael Douglas, Disney's John Lasseter, director Brian Singer, Jeffrey Tambor, Aziz Ansari, Michael Fassbender, Jeremy Piven, Gary Goddard, Gene Simmons, Ben Affleck and his brother, Casey, Charlie Rose, Woody Allen, Scott Biao, Mel Gibson, Richard Dreyfuss, Tom Sizemore, Andy Dick, George Takei, Kevin Spacey, and his replacement in Ridley Scott's movie, *"All the Money in the World,"* Christopher Plummer, Ed Westwick, Charlie Sheen, Louie C.K., Dustin Hoffman, Sylvester Stallone, James LeVine, a conductor with New York's Metropolitan Opera, for God's sake, Jim Franco and Harvey and his brother Bob, Tavis Smiley, photographer Bruce Weber, and the latest, Les Moonves, head honcho at CBS (which I suspect has to do with squabble with Shari Redstone, the controlling shareholder in both CBS and Viacom who wants to merge the two companies – the trail is set for October 3), but Hugh Hefner was a pervert too, and the Playboy Mansion was the acceptable place to maul girls.

Charlie Rose

Bill Cosby

The current (as of this writing) list of actresses, or actors, who thus far have complained or brought charges, includes Ashley Judd, Reese Witherspoon, Goldie Hawn, Jennifer Lawrence, Lady Gaga, Gabrielle Union, Eliza Dushku, Eva Green, Asia Argento, daughter of Dario, her dad, thought to be one of Italy's top horror films directors, Teri Hatcher, Angelina Jolie, Nicole Eggert, Cara Delevingne, Mira Sorvino, Kate Beckinsale Alyssa Milano, founder of the main group, #MeToo, of actresses on this list, Gwyneth Paltrow, and of course, Rose McGowan, who started the parade.

Photo Seth Wenig AP

But when another distraction comes up, an earthquake in the U.S, or a flu epidemic that causes too many deaths, a meteorite hitting the earth, or, God forbid, our president- some newspaper refer to him as "groper-in-chief - gets us into a war; sex perversion will shrink to nothingness in the news, back where it was in ancient, and now modern history. HIStory – think about that for a minute.

Let's not leave out the boys, who revealed the horrible exploitation by gay men in showbiz – Corey Feldman, Corey Haim, Anthony Edwards and Elijah Wood. Pedophilia. has always been with us. It exists in the Middle East, in the Arab countries and in Afghanistan. I read that U.S. military commanders have tried to stop the practice, but higher-ups ruled against them, saying it's a 'problem,' but to leave it alone because they 'need' them to fight the war against ISIS.

Harvey Weinstein and Kevin Spacey

Wood says his Hollywood experience is that there is a powerful pedophile ring and the town is covering up an underbelly of 100 predatory 'vipers'. Several industry agents, directors, casting agents and producers have been convicted following claims of sex abuse and former child actors. *The Goonies* actor Corey Feldman, claimed he was 'surrounded' by molesters when he was a teenager. Wood said that his mother had protected him from abuse when he first arrived in Hollywood, aged eight. 'People with parasitic interests will see you as their prey, and believes that around three quarters of child actors that 'went off the rails' later in their life had been abused in Hollywood.'

Feldman, who was one of the biggest child stars in the 1980s, was abused when he was a young actor. He said: 'The No 1 problem in Hollywood was and is - and always will be - pedophilia.' Other child actors were reportedly told by adults that it was perfectly normal for older men and younger boys in the industry to have sexual relations. Feldman told a British tabloid four years ago: 'When I was 14 and 15, things were happening to me. These older men were leching around me like vultures.' He went on to suffer with alcoholism, mental health problems and became addicted to drugs.

His friend, Corey Haim, another child actor, died of pneumonia, aged 38, in 2010. Feldman claims a 'Hollywood mogul' is to blame for his friend's death.
He said abusers are still working and are some of the richest and most powerful people in the business. It was also claimed that a number of pool parties were held in Los Angeles during the late 1990s - primarily hosted by millionaire businessman Marc Collins-Rector. At these parties, Collins-Rector and other men are said to have sexually assaulted teenage boys, according to lawsuits filed in 2000 and 2014.

Celebrities in the past have said they were sexually abused as children, teenagers, and as adults, including Rita Hayworth, seduced by her own father from the age of 12; teenage star of the 60's, Sandra Dee, British actor Tim Roth, Irish film star Gabriel Byrne, by priests in Ireland, while he was growing up, even poet Maya Angelou, and of course, Robert Blake, whose story came out in the 80's, when he was accused of murder, for which he was acquitted.

Shirley Temple says she was exposed to sex abuse as a child, at MGM, when Arthur Freed, a producer of musical films, dropped his pants in front of her. She laughed and left the room. Mike Tyson says he was the victim of sex abuse as a teenager, perhaps a cause for his ferociousness in the ring. Vanessa Williams, beautiful and a talented singer, says she was molested too. Carlos Santana joined the list – he says he was a victim of childhood abuse, and Marilyn Manson says he was also, as did Axl Rose, musician and singer.

Ann Heche says her father raped her, and Oprah Winfrey's story is well known. Not so well known is director Tyler Perry and

Mary J. Blige, who tell their own tales of youthful hurts. Roseanne Barr and Queen Latifah have been on television discussing their distorted childhoods.

Amanda Bynes and Lindsay Lohan say that growing up as a child star in the entertainment industry is no walk in the park. But some child actors experience a much more dangerous side when dealing with Hollywood's powerful higher-ups.

Molly Ringwald has written in the New Yorker about several incidents of sexual harassment and abuse in her career, including a "married film director" assaulting her on set.

Björk, the Icelandic musician, wrote that when she worked with a "Danish director" her "humiliation and role as a lesser sexually harassed being was the norm ... it is a universal thing that a director can touch and harass his actresses at will and the institution of film allows it." She meant Lars von Trier, who directed *Dancer in the Dark*, the only feature film in which she has starred.

Marilyn Monroe, despite the dumb blonde facade she portrayed, was a shrewd girl who used men and sex to manipulate decision-makers, including agents, photographers, film studio execs, directors, and a president, to get a-head in life.

The casting couch is as old as the film business, and the film business is well over 100 years old. Edward Muybridge, for his Primitive Motion Studies, from 1884 to 1887, filmed naked men and women walking up and down stairs. These images are the earliest known examples of both male and female nudity on film.

Directors have always promised young starlets jobs in exchange for parts in movies and TV shows. In Hollywood, casting couch stories are real. *Days of Our Lives* star Lisa Rinna tells of a producer who wanted her to have sex with him for a role. "I lost a role on a big TV series because I wouldn't bend over a chair in a producer's office for 'just a quickie'," Just pull your panties down and bend over and the role is yours,' he said to me."

Marilyn Monroe

Charlize Theron, Thandie Newton, and Megan Fox also tell of attempts by directors who wanted to get laid on the casting couch.

TV doesn't escape abusers and victims – Roger Ailes, Bill O'Reilly, Matt Lauer, Roy Price, Amazon studios chief, Mark Halperin, Tavis Smiley, Charlie Rose, where does it end? I remember going to parties at Cheryl Tieg's modeling agent's Nina Blanchard's house, where producers, directors, casting agents were invited to look over the line of AMW's (actresses, models, whatever), and choose who to tell their lies about coming stardom to unsophisticated young girls.

Netflix is accused of making famous teen prostitution with its new mini-series *Baby*. Baby is based on a real-life scandal of Italian teenage girls who became sex workers so they could go on designer shopping sprees. The TV show will be released this year and follows a group of high school girls in Rome who are in search of their 'identity and independence'. The series is based on the 'Baby Squillo' teen prostitution scandal of 2013. Netflix states on its website that Baby 'follows a group of Roman teenagers as they defy society in their search for identity and independence', but the The National Center on Sexual Exploitation (NCOSE) said the series is glorifying underage prostitution. 'There are no baby prostitutes, only sexually abused children'.

Bill O' Reilly

I've read that for years, Japanese teenagers have preyed on married 'salary men' to get designer handbags and clothes. I imagine it goes on in other countries.

And Showtime has *"Naked SNCTM"*, whatever that stands for, featuring Damon, who goes by one name (in case his mother tunes in), and casts him as a 'fictional' host of some private club, operating from Beverly Hills, a hangout for rich dudes and liberally stocked with babes. Damon has usually one simulated sex scene, and then cries about his mother and how he doesn't have a relationship with her – but hopes to have. I imagine the last show in the series will find Damon and his mother together – I hope it's not in bed.

And Cinemax and Showtime have soft-core porn movies late at night – must be for horny guys who don't have a computer.

Pink pussyhats are being dropped from the Women's March because they 'exclude trans women and those of color born without female genitals or whose private parts are not pink. OK, can this be the end of Rico? Those infamous words were said by Edward G. Robinson, at the end of the Warner Bros. crime saga, *"To Have and Have Not."* So, can this be the end of *this* saga? Abigail Miller, for Dailymail.com, reports that feminists are ditching the pink pussyhats during this year's Women's' Marches across the country for fear that they make some participants feel they aren't welcome. After the pussy hat-clad women filled streets around the country during last year's event, some pointed out that the pink bonnets were excluding transgender women and women of color who either weren't born with female genitals or whose genitals are more likely to be brown than pink. Phoebe Hopps, founder and President of Women's March Michigan, told the Detroit Free Press that if it makes even one participant offended, it's not worth it.

Pay to Play Auditions

When I was a theatrical agent in Hollywood, the very thought of paying for an audition was unheard of. Sure, acting coaches and teachers always said to their students that they had contacts among casting directors, or producers, or directors, and that they could get them in the door. But largely, that was a scam to get the students to pay up their weekly dues. True, most of the coaches *were* actors, and they *had* worked for producers and directors, but actors who teach are not in demand – as actors. And they wouldn't recommend their students because that might interfere with *their* getting the job.

These aren't auditions; they're called "workshops." Workshops have been around forever, but TV and streaming has increased and studios and networks don't have in-house casting departments. Workshops are being run by casting directors – who charge for them. Agents now, in a phone call, say, "you remember Tom, or Mary – they paid to get into your workshop." The Krekorian Talent Scam Prevention Act, in 2009, specifically outlaws workshops and casting directors from charging or attempting to charge an artist for an audition or employment opportunity. Since 2010, there have been *no* prosecutions.

SAG-AFTRA and the Casting Society of America say they are concerned about workshops, but both say they're unable to do anything about it - the Los Angeles City Attorney's office is responsible. A lot of money disbursed on casting by the studios is no longer spent. Actors now pay to play.

As an agent, I went to 99-seat theaters to seek out actors in plays, both in Los Angeles as well in New York. In Hollywood, no matter your role, you have influence, even if you don't know it. Warren Beatty, Michael J. Pollard and I arrived in Hollywood around the same time. We had known each other in New York before, with Pollard actually playing me, or a representation of me, in a TV special titled, *"Henry Fonda Presents The Family,"* a series of skits produced by Norman Lear and his then-partner, Bud Yorkin. Carol's role was, appropriately enough, a pregnant newlywed, which she was, with Pollard, as me, putting up with the culturally accepted nonsense attributed to pregnant women in 1960.

A couple of years later, after Warren's ascent to stardom in *"Splendor in the Grass,"* opposite Natalie Wood, his new love, and directed by Elia Kazan, he decided to do a film called *"Bonnie & Clyde,"* and took the idea to Jack Warner, legendary chief of Warner Brothers studio, in Burbank, where Warren was under contract. Warner was reluctant but was talked into it by Warren, a notoriously smooth operator.

Warren got a highly-regarded theatre director, Arthur Penn, to agree to direct it, and cast the unknown but formidable actor, Gene Hackman, Estelle Parsons, another upcoming theatre actress, and of course, Michael J. Pollard in the other roles. In a small but very effective cameo, the new to films Gene Wilder, filled out the cast. Every role had now been cast - with the exception of Bonnie. Natalie, Warren's girlfriend was his first choice, but she didn't want to do it. Warren checked out every other actress in town, professionally, of course, and wasn't satisfied with what there was to choose from. He even tried his sister, Shirley MacLaine, but she also turned him down. The start date was coming up and Warren had a real problem. He asked everyone he knew if he had overlooked anyone.

I had just returned from a business trip to New York, where I had attended an off-Broadway performance of a new play, *"Hogan's Goat,"* and was impressed by the performances. I even signed the young male lead, whose name just happened to be Bob Hogan (coincidence) as a client.

When Warren got around to calling me, I said I had just seen this play, and that the young woman in it was very talented and could very well be right for the part. I had also learned that Otto Preminger, who was casting a Columbia picture, *"Hurry Sundown,"* had been in New York, where he had made a test of this actress. I told Warren he should call Otto and ask to see the test. He did, and hired Faye Dunaway for the part. The story of the film being abandoned by Warners after it was finished, and how Warren took the print under his arm and traveled to every major city in the U.S., obtaining good to excellent reviews, thereby forcing Warners to release it, is well known. By the way, I have never met Faye Dunaway and she has no idea of the part I played in her career.

This happens more often than the average moviegoer would suspect. One of my clients in 1964 was Martin Ransohoff, the well-known Hollywood producer, who recently died at age 90. He had a script called, *"The Americanization of Emily,"* which was set up, also at Columbia, had Arthur Hiller to direct, and had signed the then very hot James Garner for the lead. Garner, just off the hit TV series, *"Maverick,"* was just starting his film career. Ransohoff had in mind a certain blonde, very buxom actress for the role of "Emily." Unknown as she was, except as a very close friend of Marty's, he was getting a lot of flak from the studio. Like Warren, he had looked at what there was around town, but needed an authentic Brit for the part. I told him that Julie Andrews, star of *"My Fair Lady,"* then currently the new rage of Broadway had been cast as *"Mary Poppins,"* for Disney, and I suggested he look at her test, because I thought she would be perfect for his picture. And she was.

I even attended plays in London, when I was there. The English, as well as Irish and Scots, have a gene for acting. They are all terrific, which you can see any night on Public Broadcasting TV. Casting directors used to go to these theatres, but don't anymore.

Agenting, in those days, one was a salesman of talent. Studio people used to laugh at my name – *"Selsman"* because they actually believed it signified what I did. But the derivation of my last name is when my great grandparents came from Russia in 1888; their actual name was unpronounceable to the guard at Ellis Island. So they asked either where you were from, as in Irving Berlin, or Izzy Moskowitz – or what your profession was – baker, butcher, chandler (maker of barrels), etc. Apparently, my great grandfather said he was a salesman – hence the name. My mother always said that in Russia, my family was horse thieves.

I used to drive to 20th-Fox, Paramount, Universal, MGM and Warner's studio offices, where I would beg, borrow or steal scripts from upcoming TV shows and movies, and read them overnight for open roles for my clients. I would then go back to the studios to sell my clients to casting directors, producers and directors. If a client was working at that particular studio, they could leave a pass for me to get on the lot. If not, Christmas gifts to guards at the gate usually worked. The only exception was Disney – Walt didn't like Jews and rarely hired them. The only way for me to get on the Disney lot was when the studio hired an agency client, who then would leave a pass for me –

ostensibly to have a meeting or lunch with the client.

Now, through Breakdown Services, you can get a list of roles open on TV shows and movies through your computer. You can also deliver an actor's reel via email. You don't even have to leave your offices. I have compassion for casting directors – true, they don't have to meet actors in person anymore, but they can get 3,000 or more submissions for roles. I don't know they handle that, but I also know the actors that they actually met – and worked with, who paid for the privilege, usually get the parts.

Porn actresses, and actors, too, are victims. Sure, they willingly perform sex acts for a camera for pay, but lots of actors in porn relate stories of being forced to take part in rape as part of their 'auditions." Jim South, the late, premiere casting agent for porn, told me that many 'fake' agents are out there, preying on young girls, and guys, causing them to 'perform' for them before introducing them to directors. Phil Marshak, a director of XXX films, and a friend of many years, told me the same stories. This was especially egregious, in his opinion, because most of these young girls and guys came from broken homes, where they endured many years of sex abuse. Many of them were drug addicts, and they played their youth and good looks for all they were worth, fading into obscurity as they aged and were replaced by a new group of 18-year olds.

Agents, too, would do anything to build careers for their young girls. I went for a weekend to an agent's home in the desert, where he gave "parties," which were in effect, sex orgies for producers, directors and casting agents. Other agents, who specialized in young boys, turned them out for the gay members of the creative community in Hollywood. The late agent, Henry Willson, represented Rock Hudson, Tab Hunter, and Troy Donohue, and had pool parties, Sundays, at his home in Hollywood Hills, in which prospective young guys were paraded around in brief swimsuits, for the selection for 'comers.'

When I moved to Hollywood... OK, Los Angeles, in 1960, Clinton Anderson was Chief of Police in Beverly Hills. He was famous for being a tough cop. The other thing he was famous for was protecting the reputations of actors. He worked with 20th Century-Fox, which was next door to Beverly Hills, and with Howard Strickling, MGM's PR head, in rounding up reporters and telling them it wasn't the way they heard – or even seen. Sounds like today, doesn't it – when the president says it didn't happen – even though there is video confirming it.

His two big cases were the killing of Johnny Stompanato, by Lana Turner's 14-year old daughter, Cheryl Crane, and the assassination of Ben "Bugsy" Siegel in 1947. He retired in 1969. Males of power have always gotten away with it since we fell out of the trees 3 million years ago. Our monkey ancestors did it, and still do it- pack mentality rules – there is always an alpha male – (and an alpha female too), in almost every species. Think about Donald Trump, John Edwards, Bill Clinton, Anthony Weiner, Mario Batali, Arnold Schwarzenegger, and on and on.

It happens in every human endeavor – finance, politics, medicine, music, science, sports, entertainment, religion, whatever –In the Mid-East, men, stronger, larger, and dominant, appear to rule, treating women as chattel, to be owned, to do whatever they wish to them. The enlightened West takes women seriously; they vote, do men's jobs in the military, run companies, earn *almost* as much as men.

But in fact, women rule. They have their own way by controlling sex, Men want to procreate, something about leaving their genes behind when they die, and women are the gatekeepers.

But the big secret, at least to men, is that they secretly fear women. Which is why they mistreat them. Not all men, but most of them. Why? Because women are smarter than men, borne out by the Minnesota Multiphasic Personality Inventory, Mensa, et al. - they feel emotions, they have to, if they are going to raise children. And because men are born of women, who have influence over them since birth. The first rejection a boy ever faces from a woman is when they abruptly pull their nipple from an infant's mouth, and he was still hungry. It goes on from there – rejection after rejection – *"don't pick up that snake, don't run into the street,* and later, *"don't play with yourself – you'll go blind."*

And it gets worse – when the young prince's testicles deliver startling erections around the age of 12, he begins to get interested in girls (or boys). He starts to pull away from mom just as she's re-attaching herself to the proto-man she believes will deliver her from her thwarted dream of equality and forever love her grown-up male partner promised her. And hasn't produced.

The young guy is experimenting, and that doesn't mean his mom is in on it. It may be that in some cases, but it's rare. In most cases, mom finds fault with his pubescent crush – *she's not pretty enough, she's not rich enough, they're not the same religion.* Mom is jealous.

Dad only wants to know if his son is getting laid. He's living his own teenage years through his son. And cautions he is too young to get hooked by marriage. Dad intimates that *his* son will always be too young to get married. Later on, mom wants grandkids. In many cases, dad doesn't – he thinks kid raising is a pain, and expensive, remembering what it was for him.

So it goes. Hollywood - promised fame, riches, and a fun existence, has always summoned pretty young girls from any country that had a film industry. It doesn't matter whether it was wherever in the world, France, Germany, Japan, China, India, Holland, England, or America – all are magnets for girls, or boys, to escape to a life of glamour. Only it rarely results in that

— more like repeated rejection, empty promises, come-on's, leading to waitressing, porn films, prostitution, and, in worst case, home, with tails between legs, occasionally with a kid, or kids.

As to old, or classic Hollywood, stories abound; Actress Joan Collins, warned by Marilyn Monroe about the "wolves" in Hollywood, also wrote in her memoir that she missed out on the title role in 1963's *"Cleopatra,"* which went to Elizabeth Taylor, because she wouldn't have sex with Buddy Adler, the head of 20th Century Fox. "I had tested for *'Cleopatra'* twice and was the front-runner," she said. "He took me into his office and said, 'You really want this part?' And I said, 'Yes. I really do.' 'Well,' he said, 'then all you have to do is be nice to me.' It was a wonderful euphemism in the '60s for you know what."

Oscar-winner Dame Helen Mirren has said that back in 1964, at 19, during an audition, director Michael Winner made her flaunt her body as he leered. "I was mortified and incredibly angry, I thought it was insulting and sexist, and I don't think any actress should be treated like that — like a piece of meat — at all."

Joan Crawford, who got her start in the 1920s by dancing naked in arcade peep shows, advanced her career by sleeping "with every male star at MGM — except Lassie," said Bette Davis.

But American culture is different from others. Actress Catherine Deneuve was one of 100 French female writers, performers and academics that deplored the wave of 'denunciations' that followed claims Hollywood producer Harvey Weinstein raped and sexually assaulted women over decades. The women said that the 'witch-hunt' that has followed the accusations now threatens sexual freedom. 'Rape is a crime, but trying to seduce someone, even persistently is not - nor is men being gentlemanly a macho attack,' explained the letter, which was published in the daily Le Monde. 'Men have been punished summarily, forced out of their jobs when all they did was touch someone's knee or try to steal a kiss,' said the letter, which was also signed by Catherine Millet, author of the hugely explicit 2002 bestseller *'The Sexual Life of Catherine M'.*

Men had been dragged through the mud, they argued, for 'talking about intimate subjects during professional dinners or for sending sexually charged messages to women who did not return their attentions.' The letter attacked feminist social media campaigns like #MeToo and its French equivalent #Balancetonporc (Call out your pig) for unleashing this 'puritanical... wave of purification'.

It claimed that 'legitimate protest against the sexual violence that women are subject to, particularly in their professional lives', had turned into a witch-hunt.
'What began as freeing women up to speak has today turned into the opposite - we intimidate people into speaking 'correctly', shout down those who don't fall into line, and those women who refused to bend' to the new realities 'are regarded as complicit and traitors.' The signatories - which included a porn star-turned-agony aunt - claimed they were defending sexual freedom, for which 'the liberty to seduce and importune was essential'. Deneuve has made no secret of her annoyance at social media campaigns to shame men accused of harassing women. 'I don't think it is the right method to change things, it is excessive,' she said last year, referring to the #MeToo hashtag.

'After 'Calling our your pig' what are we going to have, 'Call our your whore?" she said. 'Instead of helping women, this frenzy to send these male chauvinist 'pigs' to the abattoir actually helps the enemies of sexual liberty - religious extremists and the worst sort of reactionaries,' the collective of women who signed the letter said.
'As women we do not recognize ourselves in this feminism, which beyond denouncing the abuse of power, takes on a hatred of men and of sexuality.'
They insisted that women were 'sufficiently aware that the sexual urge is by its nature wild and aggressive. But we are also clear-eyed enough not to confuse an awkward attempt to pick

someone up with a sexual attack.'
On the other hand, French women are revealed to be the most likely to fake an orgasm. A third of French women regularly fake orgasms, a survey found, followed by Americans and the British. A survey carried out to mark International Orgasm Day (!), asked women from France, the US, Spain, the UK, Italy, Canada, the Netherlands, and Germany about their bedroom habits. French women were most inclined to commit bedroom fraud, with 31 per cent regularly faking with their current partner. French women also ended up at the bottom for how often they have an orgasm; with less than half saying they had one at least once a week on a regular basis. In addition, a quarter of French women did not have an orgasm the last time they had sex, and just 37 per cent of French women have had sex at least once a week over the past months. Just sayin'.

The Italians' weighed in by former, and maybe future, Prime Minister Silvio Berlusconi's comments in support of his French women friends; He insists women should be happy if men try to seduce them as he wades into the sexual harassment row. Berlusconi said it was only 'natural' that women enjoy being courted by men
'It's not an offense to court women if it stays in the realm of elegance.'
Berlusconi has pronounced that women should be happy if a man tries to seduce them. Speaking during a late-night talk show, Berlusconi said Deneuve had pronounced 'holy' words in saying men should be free to hit on women.

Brigitte Bardot attacked the #MeToo movement, claiming that most of the actresses who complain of sexual harassment are just looking for publicity. 'The vast majority are being hypocritical and ridiculous,' she told the French magazine Paris Match.

Bardot, now 83, added, 'Lots of actresses try to play the tease with producers to get a role. And then, so we will talk about them, they say they were harassed. 'I was never the victim of sexual harassment. And I found it charming when men told me that I was beautiful or I had a nice little backside,' said the actress, who became a sex symbol overnight thanks to *'And God Created Woman'* in 1956.

And for the male gender: *Taken* actor Liam Neeson told The Late Late Show in Ireland that 'famous people' are being dropped from shows over accusations that they 'touched some girl's knee' amid the scandal engulfing disgraced Hollywood producer Harvey Weinstein. His comments followed Catherine Deneuve, saying men are being unfairly targeted by sexual misconduct allegations and should be free to make advances toward women. He also spoke about actress Anna Graham Hunter's allegations that Dustin Hoffman groped her, saying: 'Apparently he touched a girl's breast and stuff, but it's childhood stuff.'

If I were in my former professions of publicist, agent and producer, now, I would be confused to think what I would do as my clients or actors came to me for advice. Relationships in Hollywood are tangled. One has an obligation to protect those vulnerable, especially young people who are unschooled in the ways of predators. I would warn actors based on what I knew, but after that, they were on their own. They were eager to meet producers, directors and casting agents, but they always thought they could "handle them." I would hear horror stories after, especially when they didn't get the job, but I didn't hear from those that *did*.

There is a bandwagon effect, in which actors and their lawyers seek to 'cash in' on the trend, threatening to go to the media if not enough cash is offered. The Hollywood Reporter says the movement has led to a rise in clients for image managers, therapists and even fraudsters. The #MeToo movement has been a job creator. The new sexual harassment 'business' also includes life coaches guiding the suddenly fired, designers making awareness accessories like the Time's Up pin and new "chief people officers," or human resources experts, brought in by companies to protect them.

One plaintiffs' lawyer says his workload is up 200 percent. Not all new business calls are legitimate; some are bad sexual harassment claims — complaints about conduct that was uninvited. In some cases, the victims' said that the conduct was welcome. A Hollywood lawyer also notes that there are many cases that have not yet become public, and 'so-called' victims are proposing backdoor deals in exchange for silence. "I am aware of many lawyers, including myself, who have received secret demand letters with disguised threats to make an allegation public unless there is a quick settlement," he says.

As a publicist, I would have advised Matt Damon and Lena Dunham to stay out of it, as they got terrible media reactions to their horning in on the subject. I read that today's publicists charge $800 an hour or $30,000 for a project for their advice. At the firms I worked for, we charged a maximum of $5,000 per month. For those rates, I may consider becoming a publicist again

The Moguls

Long before Harvey Weinstein, there was Louis B. Mayer, Jack L. Warner, of Warner Bros., Harry Cohn, of Columbia Pictures, Darryl Zanuck, Howard Hughes, Joseph Kennedy, father of Jack and Bobby Kennedy, Sam Goldwyn and Mack Sennett, and others. Joe Kennedy and Howard Hughes owned RKO, a minor league studio that Kennedy sold to Hughes. They had the 'contract," that said the studios 'owned' their actresses, and they could do anything they wanted with them. A contract with one of the major studios, or minors, like Allied Artists, or Eagle-Lion, meant you had a guaranteed income, were off the street, didn't have to waitress, or make porn films. Marilyn Monroe allegedly said, when she signed her contract with 20th Century-Fox, "That's the last dick I'll have to suck." She also described the town as, "Hollywood is an overcrowded brothel, a merry-go-round with beds for horses."

I worked for 20th Century-Fox as a young press agent in the New York offices, and whenever Zanuck came into town, I was usually detailed to accompany him, which meant sitting with him in the Board Room while he smoked a 12-inch cigar, and thought. I had a pad and pen, waiting for his thoughts. Zanuck was known as a womanizer, and as I heard it, he would work until 4 pm at the Fox lot near Beverly Hills, when he would usher a starlet into his office – and couch. Apparently, everyone at the studio knew it. After which, he'd resume work until late. Some guys go to a gym.

Short man syndrome really does exist, Oxford University academics have found, after a study showed feeling smaller makes people paranoid, distrustful and scared of others. Zanuck, Mayer and Warner were short.

Women also warned one another about the worst predators. Joan Collins recalled being a newly arrived actress in Los Angeles, at a party with Marilyn Monroe: "We started chatting and after a couple of martinis, Marilyn poured out a cautionary tale of sexual harassment she and other actresses endured from "the wolves in this town." I replied that I was well used to "wolves" after a few years in the British film industry. ... I told Marilyn I was well prepared to deal with men patting my bottom, leering down my cleavage and whatever else. She shook her head. "There's nothing like the power of the studio bosses here, honey. If they don't get what they want, they'll drop you. It's happened to lots of gals. ... 'Specially watch out for Zanuck. If he doesn't get what he wants, honey, he'll drop your contract."

Only a few days later, Zanuck, then the president of 20th Century Fox, propositioned Collins, saying, "You haven't had anyone until you've had me, baby. I'm the biggest and the best and I can go all night." Collins had no other recourse but to run. "I was so shocked I couldn't speak," she recalled, "so

I just wriggled free of his groping hands and ran back to the set."

Mayer, who co-founded MGM with Sam Goldwyn, was a little man with a Napoleon complex, who terrorized his contract actresses, saying he would ruin their careers if they didn't submit. He was vindictive, punishing their loved ones. When Jean Howard married Charlie Feldman, the agent, Mayer banned Charlie from the lot. For a long time after, he wouldn't allow any of Feldman's clients to work at MGM. Mayer's pimp was Benny Thau, the MGM casting chief, whose couch "was the busiest in Hollywood."

"Put my ashes in a box and tell the messenger to bring them to Louis B. Mayer's office with a farewell message from me. Then when the messenger gets to Louis' desk, I want him to open the box and blow the ashes in the bastard's face." - B.P. Schulberg. He was the father of Budd Schulberg, the award-winning writer, who most famous work was *"On the Waterfront."*

Mayer also groped the teenage Judy Garland, according to Gerald Clarke's book *"Get Happy: The Life of Judy Garland,"* and held meetings with the young woman seated on his lap, his hands on her chest.

Producers too, abused actresses. And so did their parents. Judy was told she's not pretty enough or thin enough, so she got a nose job and started taking amphetamines, courtesy of her mother and MGM, to stay employed.

Mayer had a 10-story building built in Beverly Hills, at the corner of Beverly Drive and Wilshire Blvd., in 1929, in which he took the top floor. Complete with 'penthouse,' up a flight of stairs, it functioned as an apartment, with a bedroom and kitchen. Mayer needed it, he said, to 'relax' away from the studio – it was a hard job running a studio. His home, which contained his wife (Cohn and Warner had wives, too), was unsuitable, since he gave dinners and parties there, and the 'help' were always buzzing about. That was where Mayer had his 'meetings' with girls who wouldn't, or couldn't say no. Donald Sterling owns the building now, and he has a reputation, too. My mother, Rose, gave Sterling the down payment in 1971. Sterling was my attorney in 1962 during my divorce from my first wife, Carol Lynley.

Harry Cohn at Columbia Pictures and Jack Warner at Warner Bros. did the same thing and got away with it because there was no one who would say 'no' to them. Harry Cohn was famous for having sex with his starlets, before he offered them a contract, because he 'wanted to know that they could stand up to anything." Kim Novak was one who admitted to it. Nancy Kovack was another. One would think Cohn had a preference for girls from middle Europe, like our current president. Nancy, who I knew, constantly avoided Cohn until she couldn't anymore – and got out, eventually marrying Zubin Mehta, when he was the conductor of the Los Angeles Philharmonic. I'm sure she was much happier.

Cohn bugged both Rita Hayworth and her ex-husband, Orson Welles. Welles caught on, and vocally greeted Cohn upon arriving at the office every day. Orson told me that story, when I was working with him for a year trying to make a movie about the assassination of Robert F. Kennedy, as well as a story about his working for a low-budget producer, Albert Zugsmith. He thought that name was funny, and when one of film students did something wrong, he'd threaten to 'Zugsmith" them.

When Novak fell in love with the entertainer Sammy Davis Jr. in 1957, Cohn ordered a mob hit on Davis, who was black, unless he left Novak and immediately married a black woman. Arthur Silber Jr., Davis' best friend and business partner, told *Vanity Fair* that Davis paid an African-American woman to marry him within hours.

Marilyn Monroe and the Kennedys

Cohn, accidently, or not, made films like Frank Capra's *It Happened One Night* and *Mr. Smith Goes to Washington*, and *All the King's Men*.

Tony Curtis told a story in his autobiography regarding Cohn which also illustrates the power that the man had. Once when Curtis was meeting with Cohn, a young starlet entered the office, wanting to speak with Cohn. Curtis got up to leave but Cohn insisted the young lady speak openly. Nervously, she prodded Cohn for commitment to his promises or she would call his wife. Cohn without a blink of an eye, picked up the phone and said "Call her". The starlet, confused and totally confused after playing her ace, left the office upset and defeated.

One joke around Hollywood was that at Harry Cohn's funeral, the people who showed up were there to make sure he was dead. Mario Puzo wrote about a fictional Cohn, played by John Marley, in *"The Godfather,"* making him the studio head, who Puzo called 'Jack Wolz," who wouldn't give Frank Sinatra the career-making role in *"From Here to Eternity."* Robert Duvall, playing Marlon Brando's lawyer, visited him and the studio head showed him his prize racehorse. The famous "horse's head" in the bed of the studio chief convinced him.

Jack Warner had his casting director, Jack Bauer, whom I also knew as an agent, as his pimp. Every agent had his new 'talent', and each of those girls had to meet every casting person in order for them to be 'cast' in one of their films. Jack knew what his boss liked, and sent the ideal girls to Warner, for a 'special' meet.

1920s Hollywood's wild stories and immoral affairs led to a blowback in the newspapers and the Catholic church. Movies were not allowed to portray prostitution, and kisses were allowed, but only with a closed mouth, and couldn't be longer than 5-8 seconds.

The hilarious moments were when two people, even though they were married, couldn't bunk together. They had single beds, even though the mass of married people slept in double beds, and when one married partner visited the other, sitting on the bed was okay, but they had to keep one foot on the ground – I guess because accidents happen.

The People vs. Fatty – Roscoe 'Fatty' Arbuckle, the 'Prince of Silent Film,' was put on trial for murder in 1921. 'Fatty' was accused of raping starlet Virginia Rappe and killing her with his enormous bulk, weighing nearly 300 pounds, causing her bladder to rupture. Fatty's case is thought to be the first Hollywood sex scandal, but we can go back further than that. Fatty, along with Charlie Chaplin, Buster Keaton and Harold Lloyd, made the moviegoing public feel good during World War 1, the Depression and Prohibition, and they earned vast incomes,, compared to the average worker. Fatty was paid $1million ($13 million today) by Paramount Pictures to act in nine movies, a paltry sum by today's actor prices, which average $20 million for ONE movie. Plus adjusted gross – and gross from the first dollar if you're a big enough name. Rappe was invited to a Labor Day party by Arbuckle at the St Francis Hotel in San

Francisco, and after drinks, according to *one* guest, 'Fatty' allegedly locked Rappe in a room at the hotel and raped her. She died four days later. He was accused of using a piece of ice or a coke bottle, or a glass of champagne to penetrate her. Fatty was so huge that he probably couldn't see his penis, much less use it. He had carbuncles, an infection that causes boils. He used morphine, which was easy to get in those days. He became addicted to it and when he drank, his usual jolly personality would disappear, and he became Jekyll and Hyde. Fatty was arrested, charged with murder and sexual assault. He was unable to get bail and so he stayed in jail. Fatty had strong supporters - including Charlie Chaplin and Buster Keaton. Chaplin's time in the unsavory glare of headlines would come later. Fatty claimed to have found Rappe in Room 1219 suffering from 'hysteria,' vomiting and trying to take her clothes off. Doctors testified that she suffered from a chronic bladder disease that would have been aggravated by alcohol – suggesting that as her cause of death. The autopsy physicians who examined her testified that they didn't find evidence of sexual assault. Fatty underwent three trials, and the jury only needed five minutes to deliberate. They acquitted Fatty on the reduced charge of manslaughter, and issued a lengthy statement apologizing to the actor. 'Acquittal is not enough for Roscoe Arbuckle,' the statement read. 'We feel that a great injustice has been done him. He was manly throughout the case and told a straightforward story on the witness stand, which we all believed. The happening at the hotel was an unfortunate affair for which Arbuckle ... was in no way responsible.' The Arbuckle case launched a movement. Women protested in the streets demanding the Fatty be held accountable for his actions. Bluenoses and the Catholic Church fomented a smear campaign against both him and Rappe, saying that her bladder was already torn by many abortions. An autopsy showed that Rappe had not had any abortions. Fatty was also demonized, with newspapers saying Hollywood was at fault, with millionaire actors getting away with murder, high living, drinking alcohol in prohibition days. There were tabloids in those days, and they went wild with the story. After the trials, Arbuckle was blackballed from the industry not just for the future, but retroactively. Copies of films he'd acted in were destroyed. He was unable to work in Hollywood. Eventually he did get a six-film deal with Warner Brothers. After going out to celebrate, he had a heart attack and died in his sleep. He was 46. Was Fatty's celebrity responsible for his acquittal? Was the fact that the moviegoing public loved Fatty, and that the jury may have been awed in his presence, a reason he got off so easily? Did the studios pay off the doctors testifying? Nevertheless, Fatty went from the top of the heap to the bottom.

Death of Wallace Reid - Silent film actor Wallace Reid, an alcoholic known in the press as "The King of Paramount," died at 31, in 1923. He had been addicted to morphine to him by the studio after a train accident on the set during the making of the film *The Valley of the Giants,* in Oregon. His wife, Dorothy Davenport, also a movie star, said that Reid's drug addiction was a disease and not a sign of his lack of morals. The story of their marriage and her husband's death was the theme of *A Star is Born,* all three versions, 1937, 1954, and soon to be a remake starring Lady Gaga.

Clara Bow - Clara had an abusive childhood – she was raped by her alcoholic father, so she had a reason to act out. She already had emotional problems when Paramount signed her. It was a time when women were feeling socially courageous, were drinking, smoking, and 'acting" like bad girls. Clara gave newspapers the weapon to degrade her. She embarrassed Paramount, the studio that had made a fortune on her, by being sued for alienation of affections by a doctor's wife. Times were different then – today she would have been celebrated for her honesty and daring. The tabloids picked up on her and reactions to Clara and to women's 'wildness' followed in the media. Newspapers continued to report how Clara misbehaved. I imagine much of it was innuendo and gossip, much like today's Enquirer and Globe stories are. And then Clara sued her former secretary for embezzlement and the secretary, in retaliation, scandalized readers with stories of Clara's having had sex with the entire USC football team, which they denied. But audiences were caught in a moment of social tradition. She had a nervous breakdown at age 26, and died alone in 1965. There were plenty of girls arriving at Union Station in Los Angeles.

The Death of Thomas Ince – William Randolph Hearst shot Thomas Ince, as he said, in the head, by mistake, aboard his yacht, in 1924. He really was aiming at Charlie Chaplin. Hearst thought that Marion Davies, Hearst's mistress, and a terrible actress, and Chaplin were secretly lovers. He invited them both on board his yacht for a cruise. He caught the couple and went for his gun. Davies' screams awakened Ince who rushed to the scene. And Ince took the bullet meant for Chaplin. If you believe that, I have a bridge to sell you in the desert. Marion Davies' secretary, Abigail Kinsolving, said that Ince raped her that weekend on board the yacht. Several months later, Kinsolving, who was not married, had a baby, and died in a car accident near the Hearst ranch. Mysterious? Two bodyguards, employed by Hearst, found her body, along with a suspicious looking suicide note. Her baby was sent to an orphanage supported by Marion Davies. Chaplin denied being on board the yacht. Published reports, remember that Hearst was the owner of many newspapers, cited "acute indigestion" as the cause of death, but rumors began circulating immediately to the effect that Ince had been the victim of foul play. Ince's body was cremated sans autopsy and no inquest was ever held. Hearst was said to have used Mark Twain's phrase when he was sued, "Don't ever cross swords with a man who buys ink by the barrel." Rumors about what "really" happened led Peter Bogdanovich to make a film about the triangle, called *"The Cat's Meow,"* in 2001.

Lupe Velez's Suicide Lupe Velez committed suicide in 1944 because she was pregnant by her lover Harald Ramond, who wouldn't marry her. A devout Catholic, she declined to call "Doctor

Killkare", the joke name for Hollywood's abortionist, according to Kenneth Anger in *Hollywood Babylon,* and downed 75 Seconal instead.

The Murder of William Desmond Taylor - The murder of 49 year-old millionaire film director William Desmond Taylor, Mabel Normand's lover, in February 1922, was another body blow to the reputation of Hollywood. He was shot to death in his LA apartment. The murder was never solved. Charlotte Shelby was a suspect, the angry "stage mother" of 19 year-old starlet Mary Miles Minter, who was seeing Taylor. Reminds me of the stage mothers of Brooke Shields, Tuesday Weld and Sandra Dee. I don't think they'd be capable of murder, but one never knows. Rumors are that Taylor was gay. A guy can't get a break – either now or in those days.

Maureen O'Hara

O'Hara, a star in Hollywood's Golden Age in the 1930s, told a story of experiencing harassment, assault and retaliation from men in the industry who nearly drove her out of the business. "I am so upset with it that I am ready to quit Hollywood," O'Hara told a paper in 1945. "It's got so bad I hate to come to work in the morning." She said, "Because I don't let the producer and director kiss me every morning or let them paw me, they have spread word around town that I am not a woman—that I am a cold piece of marble statuary." O'Hara starred in Westerns, as and classics like *The Parent Trap, Miracle on 34th Street,* and *The Quiet Man,* as a favorite of director John Ford, and actor John Wayne.

Louis, Jeanette and Nelson

The love triangle between Louis B. Mayer, Jeanette MacDonald, and Nelson Eddy is a mystery. A rumor around Hollywood was that Mayer forced MacDonald to have an abortion when he found out she was pregnant with Eddy's baby. And not *his*, I assume. In which case, he would have also insisted on an abortion. After all, Mayer was a 'happily' married man.

Nelson Eddy and Jeanette MacDonald were in the "studio system" for MGM, and were paired by Mayer for the musicals MGM was famous for. Contracts kept actors and directors, writers and directors 'virtual slaves'. MacDonald and Eddy fell in love but never married, because they were bound by their contracts, and because Mayer never allowed them to. Mayer was jealous, obviously. How dare they fall in love?

MacDonald was pregnant with Eddy's baby in 1935. They were unmarried, and were moneymakers for the studio. Mayer told the actress that if she didn't have an abortion, he would blacklist both her and Eddy, ruining their careers. MacDonald miscarried, but when Eddy and Mayer heard the news, both assumed Mayer's threats had got to her. Eddy broke up with the actress because of it. Mayer made sure they never got back together by threatening Eddy's life. Eddie Mannix, Mayer's 'fixer,' was assumed to have pushed Nelson Eddy's car off the road as a warning.

Thelma Todd

I have an unproduced screenplay left to me by my friend, Joyce Taylor Brubaker, now sadly deceased. It is strong in writing and sympathetic to Thelma. They don't make those kinds of pictures today, as audiences know. Too bad.

Thelma Todd got famous as a comedy actress appearing in films starring the Marx Brothers, Laurel & Hardy, and Buster Keaton,

Harry Langdon and Charley Chase.

Her death in 1935 was as impactful as the death of Marilyn Monroe and the murder of Sharon Tate. Todd had a speakeasy and restaurant on the beach in Malibu, *Thelma Todd`s Sidewalk Café,* which film stars, politicians, and gangsters hung around.

On Dec. 16, 1935, Todd's maid found her body in the garage, slumped over the wheel of her Lincoln. The coroner said her death was a suicide. Cause of death: carbon monoxide poisoning. Her broken nose, the bruises around her throat and two cracked ribs led a grand jury to rule that Todd committed suicide. Apparently, the grand jury thought Todd also beat herself to death. So who was responsible for Thelma's death? The suspects were numerous, as the saying goes: Leading the pack was Todd's ex-husband, Pat DiCicco, a self-described agent and pimp with underworld connections. Pat beat her. Todd divorced him. He felt humiliated and may have sought revenge.

Also suspected was Roland West, a failed director and Todd's lover. They were co-owners with West's wife in the restaurant. The three partners lived in a duplex together above the eatery. It was a strange arrangement, and West resented Todd's numerous affairs. Jewel Carmen, West's wife, was also thought to be responsible for Todd's death. She didn't mind her husband's affair with Todd, but the restaurant lost money. She threatened to kill Todd for squandering her investment.

Lucky Luciano was another suspect. Lucky was a psychopathic mobster, involved in prostitution, gambling and extortion in Los Angeles. Todd had a torturous relationship with him, which included beatings. Alice Todd, Thelma's mother, was her daughter's sole heir, and shortly before Thelma's death she announced to friends plans to build a huge mansion. Where would she get the money? Thelma never wanted to be an actress. Her manipulative mother forced her daughter, who wanted to be a schoolteacher, into a beauty contest that led to a Hollywood contract.

Loni Anderson, who played Todd in a TV movie, said, "Her movie studio and its chief, Hal Roach, also abused her. 'Hal Roach invented something called the 'potato clause. ' Thelma had a weight problem, and it was in her contract that if she gained more than five pounds, she'd be fired. So her mother started her on diet pills, and she became addicted. She also drank a lot. `Todd finally swore off booze. But the night she met Lucky Luciano at the Coconut Grove nightclub, he insisted she have a glass of champagne with him. Todd refused. Luciano insisted and ended up pouring a whole bottle of Dom Perignon down her throat. He made her take amphetamines, and Todd became hooked on the pills and the excitement of being a gangster`s moll. Luciano wasn`t interested in Todd solely because she was one of the most beautiful women in Hollywood, he wanted control of her restaurant, where he planned to set up an illegal gambling operation on the unused third floor. Luciano planned to extort powerful studio executives by having them run up huge gambling debts. Then Luciano and the Mob would take over the studios.

Who killed Thelma Todd? Officially, no one knows, but she did cross Lucky Luciano. When discussing with him the possible use of her restaurant by his mobsters, Thelma once shrieked 'Over my dead body! "That can be arranged', Luciano was heard to reply'.

The Hollywood Sign Girl

Peg Entwhistle hiked to the Hollywood sign, climbed a ladder on the "H," and threw herself down the mountain. It was in the fall of 1932. Police found her purse, which contained a note reading, "I am afraid, I am a coward. I am sorry for everything. If I had done this a long time ago, it would have saved a lot of pain. P.E." Peg Entwhistle had success on Broadway in *"The Wild Duck,"* as a teenager, and moved to Los Angeles during the Great Depression to follow her dream of being a movie star. An unknown Bette Davis replaced her. Peg appeared in small roles in some films, but nothing much came of Peg's career, much like the thousands of girls since then, who were ashamed to go back home undiscovered. "The Hollywood Sign Girl", the newspapers called her.

Olive Thomas's Suicide

In 1916, Olive Thomas met Jack Pickford, younger brother of actress Mary Pickford. Eight months later, the two were married. Jack said Olive was the love of his life, but that didn't stop him from picking up other women. By 1918, their marriage was on the rocks, and Jack joined the Navy to impress Olive and try to win her back. But how Jack planned to reignite affection from his wife when he was on a ship thousands of miles away, eludes me. Olive was a beautiful silent film starlet whose film work has been lost because early film was nitrate-based, and either caught fire easily, or rotted in some storage unit or laboratory. She died at 25 under what we'd call mysterious circumstances. Jack was a bad boy, overprivileged and a favorite of his sister, a big star then.

Jack got syphilis while away, but managed to get Olive re-interested in him, and they tried to have a second honeymoon. Jack called the room clerk of their hotel and said his wife had taken an overdose of medicine. This was 1920, and Jack made sure everyone knew he was the brother of Mary Pickford. Nobody knows what happened, but the medication Olive took was bichloride of mercury, a treatment for syphilis before the invention of penicillin. Olive either committed suicide with Jack's Rx, after she learned he had caught the disease and passed it on to her, or that Jack had poisoned Olive to collect on her life insurance policy. Olive's death was an accident, the coroner said. Like I said, Jack was a bad boy. And his older sister was the biggest movie star in the world.

Fake News (the original)

Before there were film stars, The Vitagraph Girl, The Biograph Girl, and others were the faces that appeared on movie screens as the studio's brand, much like Betty Crocker or Aunt Jemima and Orville Redenbacher are today. Hey, Orville's a real guy. Carl Laemmle, head of the Independent Moving Pictures (IMP) studio, later founding Universal Pictures, wanted a real star in 1909, and decided he had to kill one first. Carl hired Florence Lawrence from Biograph, and gave a phony story to the papers that she had died in a streetcar collision. After the public despaired at never seeing their beloved "Biograph Girl" again, Laemmle put ads in the papers proclaiming, "We nail a lie," calling Lawrence's death as what we would now call fake news, and announcing her appearance, under her own name, in future IMP movies. That started a new relationship between studios and actors that Carl may have regretted.

Thousands of young women promptly left their homes in small towns and went to Hollywood, hoping to become stars. They ended up as waitresses or prostitutes, or doing porn films, much like today, and didn't get screen tests. Actress Louise Brooks , who did make it, wrote that screen tests and movie contracts were handed out not to young starlets at the studio gates, but by the casting couch, or to women at intimate parties who gave sexual favors to influential men. She described seeing a dancer enter a hotel room with Lord Beaverbrook and "a few days later she told me that she had a contract at MGM".

A Dishonest System

It was a corrupt system, and it still is. Fearing a backlash from the media and the Catholic Church, the studios banded together and Will Hays, the former postmaster, was appointed president of the Motion Picture Producers and Distributors of America, in 1922. Hays instituted film censorship - the "production code." The Girls' Studio Club, a chaperoned dormitory for young women was supported from the donations of studios and film stars, and was created to replace the image of the preyed-on "extra girl" with the smart and well-mannered "studio girl".

such as Gloria Swanson, Joseph Kennedy's mistress, and Clara Bow had morality clauses in their contracts. The power of the studios, and their executives, was growing. The film business was becoming a moneymaker, but it was star names, because of their fan clubs, not studios that sold tickets. Louise Brooks describes it, around 1920, when the producers realized that female stars were a threat to their dominance, they waged "a concerted war on the star system," proving the power they had to make or break an actor's career. Soon, male executives were running the business, many of which not only controlled the films they produced, but the women who starred in them.

It was standard for starlets to be made over by studio bosses, with their name, appearance and ethnic identity altered. Margarita Cansino became Rita Hayworth, with a dye-job and electrolysis to raise her hairline. Lucille LeSueur became Joan Crawford after an MGM publicity man said her last name reminded him of a sewer. Louis B. Mayer named Hedy Lamarr after silent star Barbara La Marr who had died young, as a result of drug addiction. Given a new name and image, a morality clause, and publicity, including staged romances with studio actors, the star's persona were inventions of the front office. The star was a creation of the studios, and a corporate asset. They were dropped as soon as they were "box-office poison," or went against studio policy, or refused roles, or didn't 'play' with the bosses.

Rita Hayworth

I met Hayworth unknowingly in 1973, when I boarded a TWA 707 in London to return to L.A. via New York. I settled into my aisle seat next to an apparently older woman, who seemed to be mumbling to herself. I said hello but she didn't acknowledge me. Just as well, I thought, a six-hour flight and I had brought some magazines. As the drinks cart came around, I ordered a couple of Bloody Marys' and offered to help the lady on my right. She was fairly incomprehensible. She didn't even seem to want to eat, so I kept to myself.

When we arrived in New York, the flight attendant asked me if I would help the lady get to her change of planes, as we were both booked on the same flight to Los Angeles. A wheelchair and attendant had been provided, and I agreed. We made our way down the terminal to the departure gate and I saw her to her seat. I had arranged to have the seat next to her, as I was feeling protective of her at this point.

Arriving in L.A. some six hours later, I helped her off the plane, where some people met her. The flight attendant then told me I been sitting next to one of the great movie stars of my time, Rita Hayworth. Alzheimer's disease had not yet been discovered or identified as a condition at that time, and Hayworth was an early victim. She showed symptoms as early as age 42, and was 44 when I met her. She had been in Europe for a job and had begun filming her part when, according to what I later learned, she became too ill to continue.

It's only because it was confirmed that it was she, that I believed it. There was no comparison to the gorgeous international movie star, once the bride of the wealthiest man in the world, the Aly Khan; to the woman I had just spent eleven hours sitting next to. I wish I had known then, because I would have reminded her of the great parts she had played in so many American classic films, like *"Gilda," "Pal Joey," "Cover Girl,"* and, co-starring in Orson Welles' *"The Lady from Shanghai."*

Studios routinely changed the names of starlets to fit the culture of the times, which were overwhelmingly white, and protestant, making foreign-sounding names irrelevant. Cansino became "Hayworth."

Jean Harlow

The nickname 'blonde bombshell' was invented for Jean Harlow, aka the "Platinum Blond." Harlow had a bad girl and "vamp" image, which were invented by studio press agents. Her life was filled with disappointment, scandal, tragedy, and, ultimately, her sudden death from renal failure at age 26. My ex-wife, Carol Lynley, played her in a movie, *"Harlow,"* made in 1965.

The tabloids covered her personal life, which included the suicide of her second husband, producer Paul Bern, her relationships with gangsters, nude photos at the age of 17, a greedy stepfather, and a reported abortion fathered by William Powell. On screen, she caused a sensation with her easy sensuality that it led the Hays Office, the official Hollywood censors, to rule that adultery could not go unpunished.

Harlow created a public scandal by openly socializing with high profile gangsters, Bugsy Siegel and Abner Zwillman, who tried to mobify Hollywood. In 1932, already an star under contract to MGM, she married MGM producer Paul Bern in what may have been a play by star and studio to clean up her act. The marriage proved to be a sexual disaster due to Bern's impotence. Imagine being married to the world's reigning sex symbol. Probably why Arthur Miller and Joe DiMaggio failed Marilyn Monroe as husbands. Harlow then threw herself into a hot affair with her co-star Clark Gable, most likely to prove to herself, and men, *and* MGM, in general, that it wasn't *her* fault.

Two months after the wedding, Bern was found naked and dead of a gunshot wound. He couldn't get it up - his humiliation was complete. He left a note saying, "I hope you know that last night was a comedy." MGM tried to make the scandal go away, but Hollywood was consumed with it. Bern's mysterious death was officially ruled a suicide but for a time the press fed rumors that Harlow had planned the murder of her husband with her gangster friends. She survived the awful publicity and MGM organized an arranged marriage to cinematographer Harold Rosson. She was in love with William Powell, but Powell, divorced from Carole Lombard, refused to marry her, even though he had made her pregnant. I'm sure she was too nutty for Powell.

Harlow specialized in playing bad girl characters, calling them "sex vultures." In *Red-Headed Woman*, made in 1932, Harlow plays a secretary determined to fuck her way into a more luxurious lifestyle. She seduces her boss and intentionally breaks up his marriage. During her seductions, he tries to resist and slaps her, at which point she looks at him deliriously and replies "Do it again, I like it! Do it again!" They eventually marry but Harlow then seduces a wealthy, aged industrialist who is in business with her husband so that she can move to New York. Eventually, she is thrown out when she is found having an affair with her chauffeur. Harlow shoots the original boss, nearly killing him. The last scene in the film shows her in France, in the back seat of a limousine, with a new elderly, wealthy gentleman, and the driver is the same chauffeur. Audiences were wowed, and the film has been described as a "trash masterpiece. Female leads in sexual vice films were usually the bad girl or the fallen woman. In "bad girl" pictures, female characters get rich from promiscuity and immoral behavior.

Patricia Douglas

In 1937, 20-year-old dancer Patricia Douglas took a job hostessing at MGM's annual sales convention, which was hosted by comedy producer Hal Roach at his "Rancho Roachero." The party was described to the delegates as: "a stag affair, out in the wild and woolly west where 'men are men'." Douglas didn't know it was a party. After answering a casting call, she was bussed out to the desert location with 120 other young women in skimpy western outfits. It only became clear that they were to be hostesses at a studio party rather than extras on a film when they arrived at the banquet hall, and 300 sales delegates burst in. The women danced and the men eyed them up, in between eating and drinking their way through MGM's generosity. The party soon became as wild as promised, and David Ross, a 36-year-old sales executive, had Douglas in his sights. He found another man to help him force booze down her throat, then he dragged her to a car outside and raped her. "I'm going to destroy you," he told her during the assault.

When Douglas pressed charges, Ross's threat took on a new meaning. Fearing another shock on the level of the Rappe/Arbuckle scandal, MGM, and its fixer Eddie Mannix, destroyed her character and seeing to it that the studio was not named in the news reports. Douglas's crime report disappeared, and party attendees testified that Douglas had been drinking. Mannix joked: "We had her killed." Several years ago, the Coen Brothers released *Hail, Caesar!,* a comedy about Mannix, played by Josh Brolin, which sanitized both him and his work covering up this and many more studio scandals.

Lauren Bacall

In 1943, at a party in Hollywood hosted by society gossip Elsa Maxwell, Bacall writes, "I was in a short, tailored dress and sat on the steps in a corner, feeling very alone, but watching in awe the movie stars — old, medium and new — greeting each other and vying for center stage. Names-names-names, and I had to pretend to be cool. I managed until one of my heroes, Robert Montgomery, sauntered over to me. Robert Montgomery — I couldn't believe I was meeting him. He sat on the steps and talked to me — actually flirted with me. I thought him wildly attractive. It was time for me to leave; he took me to my car, asked me for my phone number. I gave it to him. He said, 'Too easy.'"

Montgomery walked off with a smirk. "He had humiliated me," said Bacall. That night opened the innocent, sexually inexperienced Bacall's eyes to the way Hollywood power dynamics worked. She hadn't been thinking of sex when she gave Montgomery her number; she had been thinking he could be a glamorous friend and a powerful contact to help her career. "That was one of my first experiences," Bacall wrote, "with the game that was meant to be played between men and women." Bacall was famed for her roles in *To Have and Have Not* and *Key Largo*, opposite her husband-to-be Humphrey Bogart.

Bacall continued writing in her memoirs; "I have participated in inappropriate behavior and banter, talking about myself and others in a way that was both demeaning and juvenile, for a quick approving laugh and a sense of belonging. Even though I was raised a feminist, until recently, I believed that this attention and "easygoing attitude" made me a "cool girl" — go along to get along. Crewmembers and actors work very long hours and people become overly familiar with one another. Boundaries become blurred; lines are crossed and personal space invaded. "Hijinks" are a way to combat the boredom of 14-hour days. That's just set life, I rationalized. But I couldn't shake the shame and confusion I felt when I got home at night. Luckily, I have never been the victim of violent assault or intimidation or rape. But the aggressive frat-house atmosphere that is prevalent in the industry can be exhausting and tricky to navigate. One way that I cope is the same way women throughout the years have — by speaking with my close female friends who have shared similar experiences. We trade tips and war stories, and it helps."

Carole Lombard

1930s comedienne Carole Lombard got annoyed with the constant harassment she suffered at the hands of casting directors and agents. Her brothers said nothing turned a man off faster than to hear a profane woman. She asked her brothers to teach her every vulgar, dirty word they knew. Men weren't just put off, they were left dead in their tracks, surprised that such filth could come of the mouth of someone so pretty and nice. "Carole picked out words and phrases she wanted to use as her weapon," her brother Fred Peters later explained. Lombard had problems with Frederic March, as did many female stars, including Claudette Colbert. Lombard had a different way of handling March, who appears to have been one of the worst predators during this time. Sick of his unwelcome advances during the filming of the classic comedy *Nothing Sacred* in 1937, she invited him for drinks in her dressing room. Not surprisingly, he took this as an opportunity to grope her, and began to feel her up — and to his shock found a large dildo that Lombard had strapped on between her legs.

Marlene Dietrich

Marlene Dietrich, another client Arthur Jacobs assigned me to, fascinated me. She was intensely beautiful and her voice was lubricious, accent and all. I had seen almost every movie she had ever made, from *"Blue Angel,"* in German, through *"Witness for the Prosecution,"* and Stanley Kramer's *"Judgment at Nuremberg."*

Dietrich, who was bisexual, wore men's clothes in public. In those days, society was against homosexuality and cross gender, and this caused public consternation. In 1933, Paramount issued a document stating that they would not allow women in men's clothes to appear in their films to end the backlash and generate some publicity. I was always a little nervous around her. Although I was 25 and married, and she was in her early sixties (she took great pains to obscure her actual age), I would have literally dived into her if she had let me. I visited her once in her dressing room backstage at the Sands hotel, in Las Vegas, prior to her nightly show and watched as she was literally sown into her silver, lame' skin tight gown.

One of my duties was to be on hand when pictures were taken of her. One such session involved the skilled Hollywood master photographer, Frank Bez. Frank and I saw quite a bit of each other because he was in great demand among the female movie stars, whom he specialized in, and Arthur Jacobs had the best list of them. Because Dietrich was no longer young, she had special requirements and, although Frank was only in his late 30s, he had studied with George Hurrell, the master picture-taker of the 1930s and 40s, who had worked with practically every MGM and other star who mattered in those days.

Frank used diffusion lenses, at times a thin coat of Vaseline, provided by Dietrich, and unique lighting that Dietrich devised and supervised, to obtain the full length and portraits he took of her. Frank also worked frequently for Playboy, and had two nude layouts in the February and March 1965 issues, the first of Kim Novak, and the second of my ex-wife, Carol Lynley.

Dietrich had a mysterious smile she would send me as though she pictured what I was thinking. I always felt my face getting hot. I learned a lot about women from her, and she knew it. God, I was in love with her.

Claudette Colbert

Claudette Colbert was unable to stop her co-star Fredric March from groping her daily on the set of 1932's *The Sign of the Cross*. According to Vanity Fair: "His hands had 20 fingers, I swear, and they were always on my ass," she recalled decades later. "I finally said, 'If you don't stop I'll walk right out of the scene and tell Mr. DeMille what you're doing.' ... So, the camera rolled again. ... Mr. DeMille yelled 'Action,' and all of a sudden I felt this hand right around my left cheek and I stopped and walked down to the camera and demanded to see Mr. DeMille!" Colbert was unable to stop March's actions.

When John Engstead was taking publicity shots for the movie, March fondled her ass. One photo, "with Freddie's hand wrapped around my rear end," Colbert said, found its way into the *Police Gazette*. "And the caption read, 'Even if the Marines haven't landed, Freddie March seems to have the situation well in hand." She stormed into the studio boss's office, and as a result, Engstead said, "She was the first star at Paramount to get approval of her photographs, and it was all my fault."

Lana Turner

Lana Turner was 'discovered' by columnist Sidney Skolsky, sipping soda at a luncheonette opposite Hollywood High School, at the age of 17. Skolsky's daughter, Stephanie, was a friend of mine in the 50's, and she told me the story was made up by an MGM publicist to benefit the columnist, and to get publicity for his 'find. ' Turner became known as the "Sweater Girl," because her breasts were standouts in the film, *"They Won't Forget,"* Wearing a skintight sweater and skirt, she sauntered along a street, spoke not one line, and was murdered in the first reel. Turner's dramatic personal life far outdid her movie life.

Mervyn LeRoy, later a client of mine at the Arthur Jacob's office, advised her to choose a catchy first name and began 'guiding' her career, whatever that means. Her acting was barely passable. By the way, Bette Davis was also a contract actress at Warners. LeRoy said about Davis, "She has no future."

In 1941, MGM fixer Howard Strickling made arrangements for Turner to have an abortion in Hawaii, while on a publicity tour. The father was rumored to be Tyrone Power. The procedure reportedly occurred in the actress's hotel room, without anesthesia. Turner's mother covered Turner's mouth to muffle her cries. The abortion, carried out by a studio doctor, cost $500. The expense was deducted from Turner's paycheck. Kind of like the way MGM treated Judy Garland.

The real story was that Turner, 22 years old, and was still a virgin when she first arrived in Hollywood. Turner found out that the expectation of young actresses was to 'put out'. And so she did.

Her mother dragged her daughter to the West Coast to become a movie star. The mother-daughter link was a contentious one, similar to the 'stage mother's' Sandra Dee and Tuesday Weld always complained about. These were women who lived their dreams through their daughters, becoming more than not, hated for their control and avariciousness over their children. Many were alcoholics. A good example of a 'stage mother,' would be Teri Shields, the mother of Brooke Shields. A New York magazine cover story said Teri had sold Brooke into Hollywood slavery, forcing her to do intimate scenes at a young age and spouting off in interviews about Brooke's breasts and her first period. Another would be Ethel Gumm, mother of Judy Garland.

Lana's wild personal life included the time in 1958, when her daughter, 14-year-old Cheryl Crane, stabbed to death Lana's lover, Johnny Stompanato, who had threatened to disfigure her. Many people believed then, and some do today, that Turner killed Johnny, and that Cheryl took the rap because she was a minor, and wouldn't go to jail. Turner's 1982 memoir, *"Lana: The Lady, the Legend, the Truth,"* focused on her eight marriages and many romances. The memoir also recalled a suicide attempt, two abortions, three stillbirths, alcoholism and her religious awakening in 1980.

Bette Davis

I knew Jack Warner is 1972. I was involved with the making of his first film as an independent producer, *"Dirty Little Billy,"* with Michael J. Pollard as Billy. Warner had recently sold his studio for $47 million, and Jack, age 80, suddenly, after 70 years, was unemployed. He had taken a luxurious suite of offices in the new Century City, and was wondering what to do with the rest of his life. Every morning, he had a haircut, a manicure, and a massage. Then it was time for lunch.

Jack L, as he liked to be called, told me wonderful and fascinating stories about his knockdowns with Bette Davis, Jimmy Cagney, Errol Flynn, Bogie, Eddie Robinson and a hundred other famous names. Jack was a terrible jokester, which was celebrated by friends and foes. He is alleged to have said to Albert Einstein, "I have a theory of relatives, too: Don't hire 'em."

Bette Davis discovered quickly what the expectations of sex were. In Ed Sikov's biography of Davis, *'Dark Victory'*, he recounts the story when famed director George Cukor dismissed her from *Yellow,* the stage production she was working in, because as fellow actor Louis Calhern said 'she wouldn't put out'.

Davis had a will of iron and her battles with Jack Warner are legendary and well documented. She also faced down her humiliations. Davis did a Universal screen test for William Wyler's *'A House Divided'*. Stepping onto the scene, with a low-cut dress, Wyler called out loudly: "What do you think of these dames who show their tits and think they can get jobs?" Wyler later worked with Davis and also had a torrid affair with her.

Davis said that Warners was her home, her 'bad' home. She was a star in her mind, and after 20 pictures, was considered a star by audiences, too. She went to Jack L., and demanded a raise, which she got, but also demanded the right to accept work outside Warners, which Jack L. refused. He would 'lend' her out to other studios, and make money doing it, but to allow her to work outside was a bad precedent – all the other actors would want it. That was the first fight that Davis and Warner had, but it would not be the last. Davis said that she was the first to try to break the hold that studios had over actors.

Davis was offered the role that made Vivien Leigh a star, that of Scarlett O'Hara in *"Gone With The Wind,"* which Warner had first optioned. Errol Flynn was to be Rhett Butler. In a nationwide poll, another publicity gimmick, Davis came out on top over Hollywood actresses. She had played the title role in a Warner's film, *"Jezebel,"* which was a giant hit, and studio execs decided that made her too well known for the role. That did it. Davis left town and disappeared back East. Warner suspended Davis for three months.

When she first got to Hollywood, she made a test for Universal, which was owned by Carl Laemmle, who ran the studio with his son. Davis was in Laemmle's outer office and overhead the execs talking about her, saying, 'who'd want to fuck her, she has no sex appeal." Davis says it's why actors like to play other people.

Davis, doing a Broadway play called *"Bad Sister,"* says that there was actor in it named Humphrey Bogart. The Hollywood execs who came to see the play didn't think he was right for movies, either.

Davis swears that she named the statuette that was given to winners of Hollywood's annual self-celebration. She was married to her first husband, Harmon O. Nelson, who had a band that he traveled with. Nelson would never tell Davis what the "O" stood for. Then he did, and it was "Oscar." When Davis was on the board of the Academy, she mentioned that the statue had the same flat ass that her husband had, and it reminded her of Oscar. Bette Davis was the first woman president of the motion picture academy.

Errol Flynn

Errol Flynn had a reputation as a 'hell-raiser'. He was a drunk and drug addict, mainly opium, and 'celebrated' for his 'womanizing' and sexual exploits. Flynn was arrested in 1942 for statutory rape of two underage girls and was acquitted. He had three statutory rape trials, and newspapers gave him the title, "In like Flynn". His career did not suffer, and his Warner Bros. contract was not affected. Kind of like the statement our current president made before the election: "I could shoot people on 5th Avenue, and not lose a vote."

Male entitlement and power in popular culture, conquering' women, then and now, is hero worship – it's what 'men do'. Three times married, he died of a massive heart attack, at 50, with his 15-year old mistress, Beverly Addland, in attendance. By his own estimate he had sex with 10,000 women in his lifetime. His love for alcohol, drugs and brawling aged him prematurely. Flynn drank two or three quarts of vodka a day. The coroner who examined him said he had the body of an 85-year-old man.

Dropped by Warner Brothers in 1952 because he was too much trouble, Flynn roamed the world in his yacht. Near the end of his life he returned to Hollywood where he was rediscovered, playing drunks in films like 20th-Fox's *"The Roots of Heaven,"* a Darryl Zanuck production, in which French singer and actress Juliette Greco also appeared. Greco was Zanuck's mistress at the time. I took Ms. Greco around to interviews in New York, when I was a young press agent for Fox. Zanuck and Flynn were drinking buddies, and Zanuck took pity on Flynn.

Flynn had a horrendous reputation for groping actresses on the set. Sylvia Sydney said that Fredric March's commenting about her breasts and body were 'playful banter.' Bob Hope was notorious for using his power to manipulate young starlets and actresses into sex. Hope had mistresses stashed in apartments in Toluca Lake, near his home. He told his wife he was 'going for a walk." He took a walk nearly every night.

Loretta Young

Young, a committed Catholic, known for going to mass every day, had an affair with Clark Gable (he was everywhere) and they had a baby, because Young knew she would go to hell if she had an abortion. Insiders knew all about it, but the newspapers didn't because of the power that MGM had. Young 'adopted' the baby, calling her Judy, and subsequently had her husband, several years later, adopt her, changing her name to Lewis. She had two more kids with Lewis, and before she died in 2000, in 2015, Loretta, hoping to go to heaven, confessed to her son that Gable had raped her.

Charlie Chaplin

Chaplin, the man George Bernard Shaw called "the only true genius motion pictures ever produced" liked young girls. Mildred Harris, at 16, gave birth to Chaplin's child. To avoid being prosecuted for statutory rape, Chaplin married Harris. They divorced two years later. He got teenage actress Joan Barry pregnant too, and when she had the baby, Chaplin was ordered to pay child support until the child was 18.

Chaplin then fell in love with Lita MacMurray, who changed her name to Grey, and got pregnant by Chaplin at 16. Lita lied to the press and told everyone she was 19. Chaplin insisted she have an abortion. She refused, and her family threatened to turn him in for statutory rape. Chaplin married Grey in secret in 1924, and said to his friends, "marriage was a better option than prison."

An original copy of the 1927 divorce papers filed by Grey turned up a couple of years ago. In the documents, she describes his "revolting" and "inhumane" treatment of her. "He wanted threesomes, and had perverted sexual desires."

One of the first films that Charlie Chaplin produced for Mutual Film Corporation, features the movie's first "gay" kiss. Chaplin is working as a stagehand. Upon discovering that one of his fellow stagehands is a girl masquerading as a boy, Chaplin kisses her several times and is then mercilessly mocked by a supervisor who believes that Chaplin is gay. The episode concludes when Chaplin kicks the supervisor.

Chaplin married 18 year-old Oona O'Neill, the daughter of famous playwright Eugene O'Neill when Chaplin was 54, and they had eight kids. I represented Geraldine, the oldest, in her film debut, *"Dr. Zhivago."* She was going with the Spanish director, Carlos Saura, and at dinner one night in my home, which I cooked paella, Carlos said he loved Hollywood westerns. So I gave him my high school captain's badge for the school patrol, which I still had, and I swore him in as sheriff of Beverly Hills.

Marty Ingles, loudmouth comic and husband to Shirley Jones, another 20th-Fox contract actress, was my lieutenant in the patrol at Forest Hills High School.

The 'bad' publicity didn't hurt Chaplin, unlike Fatty Arbuckle. In 1972, he was given an honorary Oscar.

Ronald Reagan

Ronald Reagan, the former president, was one of Hollywood's leading men in the 1940s and '50s. Piper Laurie, his co-star in the 1950 drama *Louisa*, claims that she was a virgin when she was 18. He was 39.

In her memoir, Laurie writes that Reagan was playing her father, a gentleman at first, and even asked Laurie's mother for permission to take her on a date, but instead, Reagan took them both to his house, where he made dinner. Then Reagan led her back to the bedroom. Where her mother was at that point, we can only speculate. According to Laurie, the actor was "an insensitive show-off in bed," and made sure to brag not only about the length of time he had already been erect, but also about how much his condom had cost. They must have been expensive at that time. I remember reading about the early days when they were made of lamb intestines. They're at the 99 cents store now. They cost 99 cents.

Mary Astor

Astor, most known her co-starring role in *The Maltese Falcon*, with Humphrey Bogart, Sidney Greenstreet and Peter Lorre, was a teenage silent movie actress. She was also known in the industry, like Grace Kelly, for her enormous appetite for sex. Astor kept a diary in which she related the habits, sizes, and general statistics of her leading men –on stage or off, whether she was married or not.

She was sued by her parents for financial support, and was sued by her ex-husband for child custody. The lawyers leaked part of her diary to the press. Some of the supposed "entries" may have been made up, but the public was amused or, in those days, horrified. After the trial, the judge ordered the diary destroyed. Whew.

The show must go on – and even though some parts of the moviegoing audience may have had distaste for her, Astor continued her career successfully.

Ramon Novarro & Rudolph Valentino

Novarro and Valentino were the best-known leading men of the 1920s, famous for their roles as romantics in films like *Mata Hari* and *The Son of the Sheikh*. Novarro was Mexican and Rudolph Valentino was Italian. The tabloids referred to them as "the Latin Lovers."

They were flamboyant on and off screen; actors had to be bigger than life in silent films, so talk began that both were gay. Novarro was, but Valentino wasn't. His reputation of "homosexuality" followed him until he died, and probably was the source for his not getting work in the intervening years. As far as the tabloids were concerned, Novarro and Valentino were lovers. An interviewer, probably gay, said that Novarro had secretly admitted the affair to Cary Grant.

Rumors, rumors: Valentino may or may not have gifted Novarro with an art deco model of his penis, which Novarro kept on his nightstand. In1968, Novarro was murdered by two criminals for $5,000 in his Los Angeles home. One story is that Novarro choked on his own blood after the two hustlers shoved the dildo down his throat.

George Cukor On Clark Gable

Clark Gable was masculine to the extreme. He played characters that highlighted his tough reputation, and made his casting as Rhett Butler in *Gone with the Wind,* producer David O. Selznick's dream come true. Director George Cukor was one of the few 'out' gay men in Hollywood. He was a "woman's director." Cukor was the original director on the set of *Gone with the Wind*, and was there with the film through pre-production and screen tests. Before filming could start, he was fired. Clark Gable wanted Victor Fleming, a "man's director." Gable was one of the big stars of MGM, and he wanted his role backed up by an equally tough director. He got what he wanted. Cukor knew a 'secret' about Gable, and rumor is that Gable wanted Cukor to leave because he didn't want that 'secret' to emerge.

I don't buy it. I think that Gable wanted his director to focus on him, and not on Vivian Leigh or Olivia De Havilland. Many male stars did the same, from John Wayne to Steve McQueen.

Gable's 'secret', if it were true, was that gossip at the time had Gable working as a "rent boy" before he was signed to a contract by MGM. Cukor 'knew' that Gable sexually serviced silent movie actor William Haines around 1925. Cukor and Haines were close, they had to be in those days, and that Cukor knew about the affair.

Joan Crawford

Sure, Crawford danced naked in stag films in the '20s. Lots of starlets did the same. In fact, Marilyn Monroe, in later years, was said to have done porn films. Times were tough in those days, every nickel counted. Times are equally tough for would-be actresses today. They get of the train at Union Station, or off a Greyhound bus at the depot, carrying all they have in a suitcase, and go about trying to earn a living, while waiting for that 'break.' Everybody knows those stories, they've been told innumerable times in books, magazine articles – the movies. Remember *"Stage Door,"* with Katherine Hepburn and Ginger Rogers? If you didn't see it, wait for it to come around again on Turner Classic Movies.

She hung out at the Coconut Grove at the Ambassador Hotel, drinking and participating in over 100 dance contests, winning all of them. Bette Davis commented on Crawford's many scandals. Bette Davis is said to relate another story about Crawford, "She slept with every star at MGM," she alleged "of both sexes." Crawford had boyfriends, like Clark Gable, and many affairs with both men and women, and married three gay guys. She liked, its rumored, rough sex. Howard Strickling, Mayer's PR guy at MGM, also arranged for Crawford to have an abortion, and he covered it up by saying "she slipped on the deck of a ship and lost the baby" during a filming on a ship.

Supposedly, her mother forced Crawford to work as a prostitute, do porn films and fuck her way to the top. Crawford's leading men allegedly had sex with her, along with several female stars, including Greta Garbo, Marlene Dietrich, Barbara Stanwyck and later, Marilyn Monroe.

Crawford would have liked to add Bette Davis to her list but was but was turned down by the heterosexual Davis. Perhaps that was the reason for their lifelong enmity.

Gloria Grahame

Gloria Grahame seduced her 13-year-old stepson by her marriage to the director Nicholas Ray. I saw *"Movie Stars Don't Die in Liverpool,"* the recent film about Gloria Grahame, starring Annette Bening, as Grahame. It was, I thought, brilliant, in that it gave Bening all the room to show that she is a superior actor. Grahame, who I thought at a young age, was the ultimate sexy woman, was the greatest of the 1950s film noir actresses. She won the Oscar for Best Supporting Actress in 1952 for *The Bad and The Beautiful*. Because she was a drinker, and a rule-breaker, her career began to go down. She eventually married Ray's son, Tony, and died in 1981 of cancer.

The Black Dahlia

Her naked corpse was found in a vacant lot on January 15, 1947. Elizabeth Short was cut in half and drained of blood. She was mutilated and a joker's smile was carved on her face. Short would be nicknamed "The Black Dahlia" by the press.

Elizabeth Short arrived in Los Angeles sometime during the 1940s to become a movie star. Like girls then and now, she leaned on friends and temporary boyfriends for a meal or just a place to crash for the night.

Leslie Dillon, ID'd as the murderer, was a friend of her landlord, Mark Hansen, who preyed on young girls. He let them live in his apartment, took them out to dinner, and eventually got tired of them, evicting them for a new 'find.' Hansen owned movie theatres in Hollywood, and did very well. It was before television, so people went to the movies. Hansen was also into real estate and owned apartments, one of which he was living in. Hansen told Short what he told the other would-be actresses – that she'd be a movie star. The problem for Short was that she believed him – and his problem was he fell in 'love' with her. He got possessive. And jealous.

Hansen was married, and he got in too deep. Short was double-dating him, and asking him for too much money. Dillon worked for Hansen and police speculated Hansen asked Dillon to get rid of Short. There is a scene in Shakespeare's play, *Henry VIII*, in which he asks his courtiers for 'help' in ridding Thomas More, once Henry's friend, who stood in the way, as a Catholic, of his divorce from Ann Boleyn. Someone takes him up on it and More is out of the way. Elizabeth Short's murder was never solved.

My late friend, Dick Lewis, who wrote the monthly Playboy column in which readers were supposedly to 'ask' questions. Dick wrote the answers. Dick also wrote the questions. He had a hilltop mansion in Beverly Glen, which had 6 bedrooms. He invited young starlets to hang out there. He fed them, and watched them go out with boyfriends – and got angry.

He too, had friends in the entertainment industry – among them, me. He told his choices that he could set up a meeting with an agent, me, again. I met with many girls on his behalf, always aware that he was trying to land one. I behaved. Mostly.

Bernie Cornfeld. A wealthy criminal, operating in the 60's, had a mansion which was very like the Playboy mansion in Holmby Hills. He bought it from George Hamilton. Bernie was a securities crook – he had a scam called Investors Overseas Services, with 'offices' in the major capitals of Europe. He was eventually arrested. He, too, had girls stay with him – he had one demand – that they show up for breakfast topless. Bernie's mother lived with him.

Studios Made Kids Drug Addicts

Judy Garland and Mickey Rooney made movies continuously at MGM. They'd finish one movie and start another hours later. The kids were expected to work 18-hour days, six days a week. The execs at MGM gave Dexedrine or other amphetamines to keep them going during the day, and sleeping pills to calm them down at night. That went for Ave Gardner, Elizabeth Taylor and all the other kids working for MGM

The Latter Years in Hollywood

"Real" Sex Scenes in Films

In the Realm of the Senses

In 1974, I co-produced *"Dirty Little Billy,"* with the late, great, Jack L. Warner, shortly after he sold Warner Bros. to 7 Arts, a company run by Elliot Hyman, a New York financier, and Steve Ross, whose only experience with movies was that he hired Ed Feldman, my old boss at 20th Century Fox, as head of production. Ross had built a conglomerate, as was fashionable in those days, that consisted of a bunch of non-affiliated companies such as car rentals, limousines, and funeral homes. Adding a movie studio seemed like a good idea, especially for a guy like Ross, a handsome dude and swift with the ladies. I suspect the reason that Ross wanted Warners was for the same reason that Joe Kennedy, Howard Hughes and Harry Cohn did – that was the address of nubile young girls, AMD's (actresses, models, whatever) hung out.

"Dirty Little Billy" was a flop at the boxoffice, but was loved by the French movie crowd. Pierre Rissient, who befriended Stan Dragoti, the director, and me, brought it to French cineastes. Variety called him, 'the inveterate French film publicist, occasional filmmaker, and string-pulling eminence grise of the international festival scene'. Pierre loved the film, something the French do quite seriously for certain American films - how else is Jerry Lewis explained? Pierre died recently at 79, after a lifetime of "discoveries" from all over the world. I was in Paris in

1975 on a money-hunting trip for *"RFK Must Die,"* a film that was never made, starring Orson Welles. For the rest of the saga about and Orson and me ('awesome', as he was called by his adoring crew), read, *"All is Vanity,"* my unauthorized biography.

While in Paris, Pierre invited me to a private showing of *"In the Realm of the Senses,"* a Japanese 'discovery', produced by a Chinese producer named King Hu. I was impressed – by the sheer pornography of a modern film – remember, it was 1975. Today, major studios greenlight films that are several times the X factor magnitude of that film. The director, Nagisa Oshima, shot the most gruesome collection of scenes, which were depictions of a woman whose lover dies. She cuts his reproductive organ off and wanders the streets. I guess you'll have to see it for yourself.

9 ½ Weeks

British director Adrian Lyne brought S & M onto the big screen with his film. Were the love scenes between Kim Basinger and Mickey Rourke real and not acted?

Basic Instinct – Insiders, especially the guild workers on set thought that Sharon Stone and Michael Douglas were really doing it during their love scenes.

Original Sin (2001)

Angelina Jolie and Antonio Banderas have a realistically passionate love scene that was really happening – or was it?

Sweet Sweetback's Baadasssss Song

Melvin Van Peebles said there was actual lovemaking in the 1971 film. He also got gonorrhea. His son, Mario, then 13, even lost his virginity during filming.

Pink Flamingos (1972)

John Waters' gleefully broke the rules, if there were any in those wild times, in making *Pink Flamingoes*. Divine, a drag queen, gives unsimulated head to her "son" in the film. Don't worry, the 'son' wasn't hers – Divine was a guy.

Lust, Caution, made in 2007, got a NC-17 rating because it featured explicit, unsimulated sex between actor Tony Leung and his co-star Tang Wei.

El Topo

Made in 1970 by director Alejandro Jodorowsky, is a true cult classic, shown mainly at midnight at art house theatres. I remember seeing it a private screening room, with a talk by the director. He said the scenes were not rehearsed to ensure they felt real, and only the actors, a photographer, and a technician were on the set.

Blue Movie (1969)

Andy Warhol directed this film, and it was the first movie with overt sex scenes to be released nationally. *Deep Throat* was restricted to 'art house' theatres. That movie started the "porno chic" trend. The actors 'discuss' current events, and then have sex.

Antichrist

Lars von Trier, a Danish director, is known for his 'realistic' scenes in films that he makes. This movie contains his usual sex scenes, and also includes **ferocious and anti**-religious imagery. Willem Dafoe and Charlotte Gainsbourg were the co-stars, but refused to do sex scenes, so body doubles were used. The body doubles scenes were real. Von Trier entered the 2018 Cannes Festival with a film that showed simulated child abuse. People walked out.

Ken Park

Ken Park is a 2002 erotic film. A teenager has sex with his girlfriend's mother, like Dustin Hoffman in *"The Graduate."* The sex scenes in this film are awkward, as in Mike Nichol's film, and unlike Dustin and Anne Bancroft, all real.

Risky Business

Did Tom Cruise and Rebecca De Mornay do it for real in *Risky Business?*. They were real-life boyfriend and girlfriend. In fact, they lived together. My guess is – they did. My girlfriend at the time, Helene Shaw, was Rebecca's manager, and the young lovebirds invited us for dinner. It was 1982, and I was dating Helene Shaw, a Hollywood personal manager, whose client was Rebecca De Mornay, a fast-rising young actress. She and her boyfriend, Tom Cruise, were living in a small, one-bedroom apartment on Sunset Blvd., in Brentwood. Tom and Rebecca had recently completed "Risky Business," which was his breakthrough picture, but since no one had seen it up until then, he was simply thought of a comer, based on his work in "Taps," a military school drama, in which he was an ensemble player.

Tom played a typical middle class teenager. Joel's parents leave town for a few days and he meets Lana, a hooker, played by Rebecca, who devirginizes Tom and then convinces him to turn his home into a whorehouse for one evening. Joel agrees, and while a gang of Rebecca's sexy hooker friends and randy guys turn Joel's house upside down, a Princeton University recruiter arrives to interview Joel. Joel loses his dad's Porsche in Lake Michigan, all his parent's furniture, and falls in love with

Rebecca. Woody Allen's long time collaborator, screenwriter Paul Brickman made his directing debut with *"Risky Business."* As soon as the industry saw the picture, it was clear Tom Cruise was going to be a star.

Rebecca, however, was better known and, although this can become a problem for two actors living and loving under the same roof, both she and Tom seemed very happy and very much in love. One night, Rebecca invited Helene, her manager, to dinner and, of course, Helene brought me, her boyfriend. I wasn't anxious to attend, I remember, having had a lot of experience with young actors, and thinking this was going to be a boring evening, replete with bad food, rampant egos, and rivalry between the two of them for attention.

Their apartment was sparse, as befits journeymen actors, who might be lucky enough to land a role on the spur of the moment, and have to depart for a distant location the next day. They had gone to a great deal of trouble – flowers bedecked the dining room table, wine glasses and a bottle of inexpensive Italian red wine awaited us. While Rebecca poured, we nibbled on appetizers, which Rebecca said she had made, while Tom took over the kitchen, and busied himself with a red sauce-based pasta.

I'm pretty good in the kitchen myself, so I moseyed over to check on how Tom was doing. I watched him slice garlic and onion without cutting himself, opened a large can of roma tomatoes and, while sautéing the vegetables in extra virgin olive oil, mashed the tomatoes in a bowl. He added dried oregano and basil, a few dried red pepper flakes, and a little salt. So far, so good. I would have added some fennel seeds I had crushed in a mortar, a couple of anchovies, a little sugar and some splashes of vodka, soy sauce and red wine, but then I was a guest. While that cooked, Tom broke spaghetti into a pot of boiling water, stirred it, and we joined the ladies while dinner cooked.

I was pleasantly surprised. They were cute together and I noticed the lack of competitive spirit between them, which is typical in a situation like theirs. Tom deferred to Rebecca, and she obviously adored him. I liked them both enormously. Tom talked about his strong family ties, and his growing up in the Midwest in a normal, American town.

Rebecca, though, had had a more fractious childhood. Her father, whom she had a strong dislike for, was Wally George, a failed actor, who had a late night talk show on cable television in Los Angeles. She wouldn't discuss him in public, and even on occasion, denied he was her father. Not long after she and Tom split up, Rebecca met the much older poet and songwriter, Leonard Cohen, and lived with him in great harmony until Cohen became a monk at a Zen Center on Mount Baldy, in spring 1999. Sometimes, when girls grow up either without a father, or with a father they haven't received love and acceptance from, they will gravitate towards older men for relationships.

Tom's pasta, accompanied by a shaker of Kraft Parmesan cheese, was pretty good, and Rebecca's salad, which included walnuts and slices of miniature oranges over lettuce, with a citrus-olive oil dressing, was terrific. Helene and I exchanged secret smiles, watching the two young lovers at home.

Caligula, made in 1979, was the most erotic Hollywood film I ever saw until then. It was a Bob Guccione production. Guccione was the owner and publisher – and editor of Penthouse, a rank copy of Playboy. He wanted to move into filmmaking and hired Tinto Brass, a maker of Italian erotic films. (A joke is permitted here: The word *innuendo* is the title of a gay Italian film). A lot of Hollywood actors showed up, like Helen Mirren, Peter O'Toole and Malcolm McDowell, probably to let it all hang out, as they say, and how much fun it was going to be. Guccione, who had no experience making a film, a complicated and tricky business, replaced Tinto and he gave way eventually to

Giancarlo Lui. Guccione hired Gore Vidal to do the screenplay, who must have had tons of fun writing it, as there were plenty of real group activities, including penetration, fellatio and ejaculation. Oh, and Penthouse Pets were used extensively in the film.

The Brown Bunny (2003)

Chloë Sevigny's went down on her real-life boyfriend Vincent Gallo. That's what this film is known for. Chloë was not a 'star' then.

Elia Kazan

Elia Kazan said that studio heads "thought of every film they made, no matter how serious a theme, as a love story." As a result, "They went by a simple rule: Do I want to fuck her?" Kazan explained, "If the producer wasn't interested in an actress this way, he was convinced an audience wouldn't be."

Another Unsolved Hollywood Murder Mystery

Karyn Kupcinet remains one of the unsolved mysteries that haunt Hollywood. She was found murdered in 1962, and although one of the most extensive investigations in the history of this town ensued for many years – mainly because of the power Karyn's father, the late Chicago show business columnist, Irv Kupcinet wielded, no killer was ever found. It was sad that her former boyfriend, Andy Prine, suffered career problems, probably because Irv thought he was the culprit. Those of us who know Andy, and I later became his manager, knew he had had nothing to do with it. Various aspects of the investigation turned up some bizarre theories but, like Marilyn Monroe's death, the truth will probably never be known.

On the surface, Karyn was a sweet, pretty 21 year-old Jewish girl from Chicago, who became an actress because she didn't know what else to do. Her father was able to get her a contract with Universal, and placed her under the protection of his good friend, Lew Wasserman. Universal's head of talent and contract actors was Monique James, a former agent at MCA, who quickly became ultra powerful among the soon-to-be stars. Monique didn't think much of Karyn's abilities, but did place her in guest-starring roles in a few of the 10 or so TV series the studio had running at that time.

Karyn dated around, but settled on Andy Prine, one of Monique's favorites, and a hard-working actor who mainly did westerns. Andy was a player, and had to fight off the girls. But he was also ambitious, and hanging with Karyn couldn't do him any harm, he thought, with Mr. Wasserman and Karyn's dad. After a few months, when it became clear that dating Karyn wasn't going to advance his career as much as the bigger roles he now was beginning to get, Andy tried to end the relationship. Karyn wouldn't let go, however, and became a problem. Karyn was caught peeking in Andy's bedroom one night when Andy was in bed with another girl. Karyn also left increasingly desperate messages on his answering machine, wrote him long, rambling letters to the effect of how much she loved him, and in today's climate would have been a candidate for arrest for stalking.

Her friends, including me, began to worry. Andy wasn't being nice anymore, and who could blame him. Karyn was acting strangely – not answering her phone, or her door, and being out of touch for a few days at a time. Monique wasn't putting her up for acting jobs, mainly because the producers on the lot had their choice of hundreds of more talented young women, and it wasn't improving their prospects with Lew if they hired her, either. One night, Bobby Mirisch and I, and our wives were out to dinner, and decided that he and I would go over to Karyn's apartment when we were finished, to see if she was there. We sent our wives to the Mirisch home on Elm Drive, in Beverly Hills, to wait for us. Bobby and I parked on Fountain Avenue, a little east of La Cienega, in West Hollywood, and walked up to her door. We could hear the TV on, and through the closed blinds, see blue light seeping out from the TV picture. We knocked, then pounded on the door and called out her name. No answer. It occurred to me she might be entertaining, so we left.

The next day, I was shocked to hear that Karyn was dead. Apparently her parents, in Chicago, became sufficiently worried to call another of their friends, publicist Henry Rogers, of Rogers & Cowan, who got a deputy sheriff to open the door. She was found naked, grotesquely sprawled on her couch, her head askew at an impossible angle. She had been dead, apparently, some three days. I was told the stench was awful.

The autopsy concluded from the broken bones in her neck that she had been strangled – by someone left-handed. Andy Prine was not left-handed. The Kupcinets' flew out and immediately retained private investigators to aid the LAPD. A great deal of pressure was put on the police, not only by the media, but also by the film community and Lew Wasserman. Despite Andy having had an alibi, he was immediately considered the top suspect. Mainly, I think, because the Kupcinets' had never liked him.

The private investigator and not the local police turned up an appalling theory for Karyn's death. Unbeknownst to us, her closest friends, and Andy, her most recent boyfriend, Karyn, evidently, was living a double life. Long before cocaine and heroin became commonplace in Hollywood, Karyn was into it, and she was hooked. In addition to her steady fifteen hundred dollars per week studio contract, Karyn also received another thousand as allowance from her folks. Twenty-five hundred per month in 1962 was a queenly amount of money. But not enough, it seems, to support her habit. The P.I turned up dozens of potential suspects. Karyn would frequent a Santa Monica Blvd. bar & grill called the Rain Check Room, in West Hollywood, near her apartment, and would bring guys back for quickies, for the money. Also identified were service people, including a TV repairman, even a UPS deliveryman, who had been seduced by Karyn. They were all checked for alibis, and whether or not they were left-handed. The inquiry expanded until there were almost too many potential suspects to make a coherent case. Nothing conclusive was ever determined, and the Kupcinets returned to Chicago to grieve. There can be no worse punishment for a parent than to lose a child in such a horrible way.

Assumed Sex Scenes in Films

Writers and directors came up with ingenious ways of simulating sex both in the early days, and later in the 50's, up through the 80's, when naked bodies and simulated sex appeared on screen. A couple would embrace - cut to a scene of crashing waves, or in *"To Catch a Thief,"* just when Cary Grant and Grace Kelly were about to 'do it,' cut to fireworks over Monte Carlo. I just saw, for probably the 20th time, Hitchcock's *"North by Northwest,"* starring one of his favorites, Cary Grant – this time with one of his ubiquitous 'blondes,' Eva Marie Saint. Just when the movie is approaching its climax, Grant and Saint are too. The last scene is a train going into a tunnel. Another assumption, especially in westerns, was that bar girls, or saloon girls were a manqué for prostitutes. Don't tell me that Miss Kitty, who was Matt Dillion's girlfriend in *"Gunsmoke,"* my favorite TV series when I was a kid, was a hooker. She was, but don't tell me.

I was making films in the 1970's in various states that had right-to-work statutes, meaning unions weren't required, other than Screen Actor's Guild. Charlie Pierce, the director, and I made five movies in places like Montana, Florida, Arkansas, and Texas. Charlie fancied himself the artistic inheritor of John Ford, the iconic director of westerns, and the 'discoverer' of John Wayne. So he made two westerns – but they weren't about cowboys and Indians, they featured 'trappers' and Indians, approximately 100 years earlier. There were bar girls, or saloon girls in *"Winterhawk,"* and *"Grey Eagle,"* both of which were filmed in Montana. They are beautiful to watch, given the spectacular grandness of Glacier National Park.

A not-so-funny incident occurred during the making of "Winterhawk." The film called for a dance hall crowded with at least six easy women of the time. I had a brilliant idea, and called my friend, Marilyn Grabowski, who headed the photography department at Playboy. Playboy, at the time, had a modeling agency, another income stream for Hefner, and Marilyn suggested I interview a dozen or so of the girls, and make my selection. The first pictures I had seen of them were nudes, and seeing them dressed threw me somewhat off. I chose six girls, made the financial arrangements with Playboy, and booked Charlie's plane from LAX to Kalispell for the next week.

We all met up at 6 a.m., at Van Nuys airport, in the San Fernando Valley, settled in on the plane, which sat eight, including the jump seat, which covered up the on-board toilet, and took off for Salt Lake City, as far as the Mitsubishi MU-2 would go without fueling up again. Charlie had employed a new pilot, a young man of 21, named Tom, whom I had not met before. He looked even younger than his age, and his hands shook peculiarly on takeoff. Was I worried? – Not. Until two of the girls produced joints, which they immediately lit up and passed around. Charlie, ever the genial host, had stocked the plane with champagne, which was also opened, and passed around.

The cabin of an MU-2 is about the size of a stretch limo, and the marijuana smoke was affecting everyone, including the pilot. Was I worried? – I was beginning to be. Tom wondered why the cigarettes the girls were smoking smelled so funny. It was obvious this was new to him. Great.

All that champagne quickly got to everyone's bladder during the four-hour trip to Salt Lake, and the jump seat became everyone's best friend. In such close quarters, with six gorgeous women peeing right next to me, we all naturally became very good friends. As much as I tried to hold it in, I couldn't, and thanks to the razzing I got from the girls, it was my turn. Naturally, I had to stand up. I told Tom to hold it steady, as there was no room to spare. I had received compliments before, but never until that moment, did I experience such complete approval from six women who knew what they were talking about. Life was good.

We reached Salt Lake airport, somehow, and the girls dashed off to a proper restroom, while Tom oversaw the fueling and checked the tire pressure, the oil pressure and the rest of the checklist. The girls and I ate breakfast in the airport coffee shop, and brought a sandwich and coffee out to Tom, who looked like he needed the coffee.

An hour later, we were airborne again, and while crossing the mountains of Utah, Tom suddenly said, "What the hell...." "What's the problem?" I asked him, since I was now seated in the co-pilot seat. "We're out of gas," he said. "How could that be?" I asked, "We just gassed up." "I don't know," he said. Of course the girls heard this, since we were as jammed in the cabin as we would have been in a car, and all of a sudden, everyone sobered up real fast.

"What are we going to do," I inquired? "I don't know," said Tom, "probably look for a place to set down." "Set down," I asked? "Where?" We were past the mountains now, crossing over the corner where Idaho and Wyoming touch, and approaching Montana, which luckily is pretty flat in that area. The gas gauge read empty and one engine was coughing, but not as badly as I was from the pot and from fear. Tom selected a long, flat, empty ranch road, and we glided down on one engine and made a perfect 3-point landing. The fuel had been sucked out by the wind because the service people at the Salt Lake airport had not fastened the fuel cap securely, and Tom had not personally checked it. I guess it was the grass we had smoked. We were in the middle of nowhere and this was before the cell phone era. There I was, in the middle of nowhere with six incredibly beautiful girls in various states of consciousness. What to do.

We had seen a couple of farmhouses on our way down so, devilishly, I thought, I dispatched three teams of two Playboy models each up and down the road, with instructions to obtain a telephone and call in our problem and location. Tom and I chuckled, imagining some rural farmers answering their doorbell and seeing an apparition from another world. The girls all scored and were warmly received by their hosts, some of which were youngish men who didn't want them to go. Charlie sent his bus for us and we took off for Kalispell with no further adventures. Boy, were we glad to get there.

Gore Vidal

Gore Vidal said of Grace Kelly: "Grace almost always laid the leading man . . . She was famous for that in this town." I've not seen reports about Kelly and Cary Grant. If I were Grace, I wouldn't let him get away. And perhaps she didn't.

Natalie Wood – Accident or Murder?

After all this time – why has the Sheriff's office re-opened the Natalie Wood case? Most insiders who knew them, in my time, accepted the story that "Nat", as she was called by her friends, drunkenly tried to get into her boat's dinghy in Catalina harbor, and missed her footing, ending up in the water. I knew both, because they were represented by Guy McElwaine, who was a partner in the Arthur Jacobs office, and RJ was under contract to 20th-Fox. She, her husband, "RJ," who's better known by his real name, Robert Wagner, and Chris Walken were all drunk, as related by the restaurant staff, and RJ and Nat's boat captain After an argument between and RJ and Walken, either she snuck out to have a rendezvous with Walken, or who knows what, and RJ was sleeping, or as reports recently have it, the boat captain, Dennis Davern, and Nat's sister, Lana, have said, RJ saw her fall in the water - and refused to help her.

RJ has been named as a person of interest in the death of his late wife Natalie Wood. I suspect that it has to do with the broadcasting of the CBS Special, which purports to 'investigate" her death. There have been lots of investigative TV shows that re-hash old 'mysterious' deaths of well-known people, a result of the 'reality' wave of inexpensive shows that use a minimum of writers, and rely on old footage shot years ago. I know, because I'm the last of those functionaries who actually worked with some stars, mainly Judy Garland and Marilyn Monroe, and I've been interviewed by TV shows in the U.S. and Europe. Some readers might have watched the TV show about Gianni Versace and his murder.

I knew Lana Wood, too, in the 80's because she wanted to sell a book about her sister's 'murder,' and I was the literary agent at the Lew Weitzman Agency, in Beverly Hills. We had no luck selling the book, mainly because no one bought the story she was peddling. I read recently that Lana, broke, was living in a run-down motel in the Valley, with her two kids. 15 minutes of fame, and CBS money, for Lana and Davern.

How the Term "Blowing Smoke" Came About

Stevie Nicks, lead singer of Fleetwood Mac, was cocaine addict. In fact, she bought $1 million worth of cocaine and it burned a hole in her nose the size of a dime. She started having nosebleeds, falls on stage, blackouts and near overdoses. The rumor is that she had a 'personal' assistant blow the drug up her ass.

Roman Polanski

Polanski was pitied when his pregnant wife was murdered by Charlie Manson's gang. But he was reviled in the media, and by the industry, when he was charged with raping a 13-year old girl, after feeding her a Quaalude and wine.

Polanski pleaded guilty to unlawful sexual intercourse with a minor. He had served a number of days in jail, and was allegedly told by a judge that he had served enough time. That wasn't the way the judge heard it, and was about to sentence Polanski to prison. Polanski was a hot director then, having done *"Rosemary's Baby"* and *"Chinatown,"* for Bob Evans at Paramount. He was also a friend of Jack Nicholson, who played the lead in the latter film. So Polanski was 'lawyered up," as the saying goes. He was out on bail, and he skipped, in bail terms, to his home in France. – never to return to the U.S. Successive courts have tried to get him back, but no dice. He was arrested in Switzerland, where he had moved, while his potential extradition was discussed. But he beat that rap too, and remains a free man in Europe. The 13-year old girl, Samantha Geimer, even pleaded for charges to be dropped against him, but she was refused. In 2003, Polanski was given an Oscar for directing "The Pianist" at the 75th Academy Awards—the admitted child rapist received a standing ovation. Charlie Chaplin got one too, even though he was known as a child molester.

Maria Schneider

Maria Schneider who starred alongside Marlon Brando in 1972's *Last Tango in Paris*, said she was "humiliated and 'a little raped'" by director Bernardo Bertolucci. The director and Brando didn't tell Schneider about the use of butter in the anal rape by Brando of Schneider. "I wanted her reaction as a girl, not as an actress. I wanted her to react humiliated," said Bertolucci. Schneider later committed suicide.

Charlie Sheen

I remember, in 1993, when Heidi Fleiss was arrested for running a prostitution ring. Some of my friends were worried that their names would be in Heidi's black book. Charlie Sheen's was. Sheen, a bad boy, was notorious for drugs, alcohol, and catting around with questionable women, even though he was married, and had adorable children. He had been an authentic movie star, co-starring in Oliver Stone's *Platoon,* and with Michael Douglas in *Wall Street.* TV star is the next best thing to being a movie star, so when Hollywood turned against him as he became uninsurable, he signed with CBS for *Two and a Half Men,* which became a hit. He was the highest-paid actor on TV. I should ask him to buy my lottery tickets – he is that lucky. Fleiss was sentenced to thirty-seven months in prison, but not for prostitution – it was for tax evasion, the same charge that got Al Capone sent up the river.

Linda's Story

Linda Bloodworth-Thomason is the creator of *'Designing Women'* and Bill and Hilary Clinton's confidant, and she tells horrific stories of sexual impropriety and abuse of power. "The No. 1 casting criterion for an actress is that she be 'hot and fuck-able".

Alfred Hitchcock,

Alfred Hitchcock was well known for having a "type." "Blondes make the best victims," he said. "They're like virgin snow that shows up the bloody footprints." The blond star of The Birds and Marnie, Tippi Hedren, wrote in her memoir that Hitchcock victimized her, throwing himself on top of her and groping her, then punishing her on set for resisting his advances.

Deep Throat

One can't give a history of sex in Hollywood without *Deep Throat*. It was a movie, sure, but everybody who 'knows' knows it was a mafia investment. It was, or it wasn't, but it signified a clean break of what was acceptable to show in theatres. Linda Lovelace, the star, had a unique ability – to engorge a large man's penis in her mouth – in this case, Harry Reems, possessor of the biggest penis then known to man. Or woman. Some say that John Holmes' was bigger, at 13-1/2" long, but exaggeration is popular these days – the biggest inauguration crowd, the biggest tax cut, etc. It became part of the social fabric – *"All the President's Men,"* starring Robert Redford and Dustin Hoffman, playing two Washington Post reporters, Carl Bernstein and Bob Woodward, used 'deep throat' as the name of their contact, who revealed the names of the Watergate thieves, leading to the resignation of President Nixon. There are some people who hope for another, similar event in the near future. But I digress.

Self-identified Hollywood pimp Scotty Bowers, in his highly suspect auto- biography, tells a story about director Tony Richardson and Linda Lovelace's Oral Sex Presentation. Richardson was a famous director in the 1960s. and was incredibly taken by porn star Linda Lovelace after her first and most iconic film, Deep Throat. So taken, in fact, that he wanted Bowers to arrange a meeting between them so he could learn more about her talent for performing fellatio. The two did end up meeting, and Tony paid to book Lovelace for a party he arranged for some of gay Hollywood's top movers and shakers. The lecture apparently went pretty well. Linda showed up with a big latex dildo to demonstrate some of her moves, and some guests even went up to her afterward to trade tips.

Rumors

Scientology is said to have pictures of Tom Cruise and John Travolta, which is how they keep them under control. What those pictures consist of is anybody's guess.

Cary Grant and Randolph Scott supposedly were more than just roommates when they shared a house together in the 1940s.

Dorothy Dandridge

Ingo Preminger, an agent turned producer, told me that his brother, Otto Preminger, the bombastic German film director, had directed Dandridge in *Carmen Jones*, which made her a star. When she became pregnant by him in 1955, he wouldn't marry her. Otto was a white man. Dandridge had an abortion.

Teresa Russell

Theresa Russell says producer Sam Spiegel allegedly tried to force himself on her in her first casting session for *"The Last Tycoon."* She got the part, but Spiegel said she 'would never work in Hollywood again. She got even by marrying director Nick Roeg, and starring in many movies thereafter.

Lesley-Ann Down

Spiegel again - English actress Lesley-Anne Down recalled: "I went up to his suite, and before I'd even said hello, he'd stuck his tongue in my mouth. "

The Shoebox

Speaking of Polanski, Robert Evans, former playboy, model and dreadful actor, was made head of Paramount Studios production by Charles Bluhdorn, who bought the studio to meld with his battery manufacturer, chrome plating company, and several others, in what became the first conglomerate since the Roman Empire – Gulf + Western Corp. Evan's new post was a mystery to Hollywood insiders, whose experience with studio heads usually involved actual producers with multiple credits to their names.

Evans had been to Hollywood many times before – he was 'discovered' in a swimsuit at the Beverly Hills Hotel pool, by 30's film star Norma Shearer, who was a consultant to MGM in their search for an actor to play her late husband, Irving Thalberg, then head of production for MGM, in the film about Lon Chaney, one of early cinema's most noted stars. Evans, as was Thalberg, is Jewish, slim, with straight black hair, and looked – from a distance, like the former MGM executive.

Evans took to the Paramount job with full force – and got exceedingly lucky – he backed Francis Coppola in the film adaptation of *"The Godfather,"* an enormous hit. Evans followed that up with Roman Polanski's *"Rosemary's Baby,"* again, a monster at the boxoffice. Polanski then directed *"Chinatown,"* starring Jack Nicholson – once more a winner in theatres. Evans, Polanski, Nicholson and the addition of Warren Beatty, became fast friends and co-conspirators in women, usually young, always beautiful.

The rumor is that a messenger would arrive every Friday evening at Evan's mansion in Beverly Hills, with a 'package', intended for 'Evan's eyes only', from the major actor's and model agencies, of the arrival of any young, beautiful and new entry into the wanna-be movie star race. He wanted statistics and photos of these nubile girls. Which he kept in – a shoebox.

Upon consultation with his friends, including Beatty, Polanski and Nicholson, the prospects would be divided, with Evan's getting the pick of the litter, and leaving his friends to squabble it out for the remaining 'talent.' The fortunate young things would receive an invitation to Evan's home for a 'pool party'. The pool parties were famous in certain circles – they were replete with cocaine and sex. Some privileged girls were invited to stay in the pool house, which had several designations; 5-Star, and descending to 1-Star. A certain Secretary of State, when he visited, always got the 5-Star suite. Many young women went home to Iowa or Idaho worse for their wear, but sometimes a girl could get lucky and become a movie star, like Raquel Welch, and Michelle Pfeiffer, who was a 'tenant' for some months, and earned her keep by doing Evan's laundry.

Evans, at 86, is a cocaine addict, had several strokes, and reportedly, is an invalid. He still has that shoebox, I am told.

Jack Ryan

I knew Jack Ryan, and went to parties at his house in Bel Air. He was the 'inventor' of *Barbie*, the doll, and *Hot Wheels*. He was rich, and the underbelly of showbiz took advantage of him. He married Zsa Zsa Gabor, and was crazy about Hollywood. He was crazy in the psychological sense, too. He would throw the most debased parties, complete with drugs, expensive wines and liquors, and invited 'starlets', some off the street on Hollywood Boulevard, greeting them by lying in a coffin, masturbating. He was the "B" version of Hugh Hefner.

Cults in Hollywood

I met Andrew Keegan, an actor who was in *Party of Five*, a TV series long gone, at "The Expo," held three years ago at the Los Angeles Convention Center. Keegan founded a spiritual cult called *Full Circle*. I actually attended a session, held on Sundays, at a little house he rented on Rose Avenue, in Venice. Girls outnumbered boys, which is how you know it's a cult. The young people sat in a circle, on the floor, while Andrew (you were not allowed to call him "Andy") preached. I call it preaching because that's what he was doing. He was an actor, and knew how to modulate his voice and gestures for the effect he wanted. I assume he wanted to control the girls – as any self-respected cult leader would.

Hollywood history is replete with the allure of cults: the Manson family to Scientology. Hollywood attracts young people from all over, from questioning religious types, to runaways, to mid-country beauty contest winners, to rebels from their families. The similarities involve looking for answers to the hole in their personalities. The mystery of cults is they're all the same, whatever they call themselves. I know perfectly sane people, if actors can ever be called 'sane,' who belong to Scientology, for instance. Charles Manson belonged to Scientology, where he met his 'family." I remember Rajneesh, in the 1980's, who preached free love, and had 64 Rolls-Royces, and started Rajneeshpuram commune in Oregon, where his adjutants tried to take over a small town, and didn't get their way, so they attempted to poison the town's water.

The latest is Nxivm, similar to the religious cults, led by a guy, Keith Raniere, who wanted to fuck as many girls as possible, so he had Allison Mack, an actress, act as his pimp, luring unsuspecting other girls into a relationship with him. Nxivm has announced, "with great sadness," that they are not taking new members at this time. Of course they are not because Raniere has been arrested and faces a multitude of criminal charges.

The Kiwi Reports why most studios don't want to work with these A-list stars

Charlie Star, in the April 9, 2017 edition says that **John Travolta** has been part of some of the most profitable films in Hollywood history, including *Pulp Fiction*. He was nominated for an Academy Award for his performance in the movie. However, he was also involved in some less hit projects which hurt his reputation as an actor. The *Grease* star has become too big of a chance for Hollywood producers and they think twice before casting him now to different films. That, and his being a proud supporter of Scientology. My client, when I was an agent, was Diana Hyland, who became a TV star in the television version of *"Peyton Place."* She and Travolta had had a passionate affair several years back. Diana was almost twice his age.

Jim Carrey finds himself on this list, as studios don't know if Carrey will be loved or hated in a film, it's a complete toss-up and they aren't willing to take the risk. Carrey has been out of the spotlight for quite a while due to personal issues.

Steven Seagal is not only arrogant and self-centered, but it has been rumored that he tends to lie. Seagal who was also banned from the sketch comedy show, Saturday Night Live, has been outed as a female abuser. Seagal, before he was an actor, was a personal trainer to Mike Ovitz, one of the founders of Creative Artists Agency, a powerhouse theatrical agency. Ovitz, on a bet, said he would make his personal trainer a movie star. He succeeded, at least for a while.

Adam Sandler's reputation in the film industry has rapidly dwindled over the years, as a result of his mood swings and misunderstood, abstract creative vision. Sandler has severe difficulty finding roles outsides of his own projects. Besides, even his own Happy Madison pictures haven't been doing so hot with the critics that have agreed to watch them.

John Malkovich

One of my favorites as an actor, Malkovich is one of the most unique characters in Hollywood. Among the films he has appeared in was *Being John Malkovich*. Imagine that – a film about an actor playing himself. He has a debatable personality and a reputation of someone who is difficult to work with. In the past he has gotten into heated confrontations on set and off of it. Malkovich also has a certain typecast which makes it hard for studios to cast him in different roles.

Bruce Willis

Willis is said to be very hard to work with because he is very unapproachable while on set. He doesn't like being talked to and focuses on his role entirely without distraction. Director Kevin Smith went so far as to calling Bruce "soul crushing" to film with on the set of *Cop Out*. Leave Bruce alone!

Tom Cruise

There's more than a slight decline in the studios' and audience's interest in Tom Cruise and his *Mission Impossible* films, recently. Outside of the action films he's best known for, unless he works with a top director, like Steven Spielberg, his films usually flop at the boxoffice. That's why Paramount keeps coming back to *Mission Impossible* – what is it – ten? His reputation of being overly-controlling on set and in his personal life did not help. His affiliation with Scientology – he had a tent set up with Scientology staffers and literature on several film locations, causing other actors he was appearing with, uncomfortable. For those reasons, the studios think twice when it comes to signing contracts with Cruise.

Gary Oldman

He won an Academy Award for Best Actor for portraying Winston Churchill, in the *"The Darkest Hour,"* but studios and fans are still smarting over his defense of Mel Gibson, who rants against Jews and women, and is a perpetrator of abuse of women. Oldman has been blacklisted from movie studios over the past several years due to his "misogynistic outbursts" against Nancy Pelosi. The motion picture industry was started by Jewish people, and much of the executive posts remain among Jews.

Julia Roberts

Roberts was acting like a total turbulent diva, according to Steven Spielberg, during the making of the film, *Hook*. Spielberg nicknamed her 'Tinkerhell'. You don't mess with Spielberg. He and Roberts have not worked together since.

Dustin Hoffman

Hoffman's reputation as a 'star who is difficult to work with' comes from the fact that he pretty much drives everyone crazy on set. He was recently outed as a sex abuser by several women who worked the sets of his films, claiming that he either laid hands on them, or, worse, that he tried to 'get close" to them, whatever that means. Hoffman apparently forgets what his role is on set.

Mickey Rourke

Rourke admitted more than once that he was difficult to work with. When he was asked once about his chance at getting an Oscar he said: "Well, I don't know, it's voted for by people from the movie business and in the past I've pissed them all off. I was good at that. It came easy to me. 'I stupidly said acting wasn't a job for a real man. I threatened producers, raged at directors, forgot my agent's name. I really burned my bridges. And a lot of people have long memories."

Joaquin Phoenix

Joaquin Phoenix has always been a little different, to say the least, in terms of his stardom status and overall behavior, compared to his fellow Hollywood stars. His eccentric behavior could be interpreted as something totally wrong, however his attitude did cost him some major roles. He was considered for the part of the Joker in *Suicide Squad* or for the leading role in *Doctor Strange*. Sounds like typecasting to me. He's also known for dragging film contracts and negotiations out for months, causing delays in filming.

Jared Leto

Leto must have idolized Daniel Day-Lewis, because once he gets a role, he stays in character throughout the shoot – and for sometime after. He thinks actors don't break character, not even for a second, even if they are not being filmed. When you're working on a movie set with other actors and actresses, especially other famous ones, it could be perceived as quite annoying and even arrogant in a way. Imagine you're playing a serious role and then staying in character when the cameras are not rolling.

Jennifer Aniston

Aniston's movie career is unusual in that most of her films fail at the boxoffice. Yes, she was a TV star, but that doesn't guarantee people will pay to see her up on the big screen. Besides, she isn't friendly to other actors. She was infamous for isolating herself from the rest of the cast, and used to eat alone at breaks on movie sets while the rest of the cast was eating together. The actress also demands that her private hairdresser travel with her everywhere she went, which studios reject unless of course, you are making money for them.

Tobey Maguire

Maguire is said to be a true pain in the rear during filming and a male diva, also. A casting director called Maguire "the worst little monster you've ever met" and is said to rain terror on anyone who looks him directly in the eye behind the scenes of a film. The worst, however, was when during a poker game he told one of the hostesses to "get up on that desk and bark like a seal." Outside of *"Spiderman,"* what pictures, starring him, have done "boffo" boxoffice?

Brendan Fraser

Fraser's just not a safe investment anymore. His acting skills tend to cost more money than they actually make in return. His choices are self-defeating – after all, he chose to appear in *Extraordinary Measures* and *Furry Vengeance* and *Monkey Bone*. He's lost all credibility with his former audiences.

Taylor Lautner

Lautner, a TV actor, one of a multitude of actors in the *Twilight* saga, had begun making out of control monetary demands when discussing potential film contracts, and no director or producer felt he was worth that $7 million he kept insisting on. After the vampire – werewolf series ended, he tried his hand at the action genre but fell flat.

Hilary Swank

Hilary Swank may be one of the greatest actresses of our time. With roles like *Boys Don't Cry* and *Million Dollar Baby*, she proved just how worthy of that Oscar win she was. Now, Swank has barely made an appearances in major projects. It's possible that she either got as far as she could a few years or back, or maybe, just maybe the Academy Award winner is satisfied with what she's accomplished this far. Regardless, the demand for a movie starring Hilary Swank is almost non-existent.

Vince Vaughn

One would have expected Vince Vaughn to stay in the spotlight longer than he has. After all, he starred in several films that did well at the boxoffice, among them *Wedding Crashers* and *The Break-Up,* featuring Jennifer Aniston, but after these two films became a thing of the past, so did Vaughn. He's regarded as a one-dimensional actor who plays the same character type consistently.

Rob Schneider

Rob Schneider is usually thrown a bone by his buddy Adam Sandler whenever you see him a new movie. As funny as he is, he never had what people in the biz call "star quality." Schneider's off-screen opinions have given him a sour reputation. The comedian has been publicly criticized for his anti-vaccine stance and ripped to shreds for always playing ethnic stereotypes in films. He's being punished by the industry by doing voice overs for children's flicks.

Macaulay Culkin

The child star turned train wreck is genuinely talented and his substance use problems have stood in the way of his acting for a long time. Hollywood won't cast Culkin anymore because of his personal problems and consequent erratic behavior.

Eddie Murphy

Eddie Murphy's personal life is a factor in his recent lack of work. Murphy engaged in a heated legal battle with Scary Spice over the paternity status of their child and the fact that he's fathered several children with multiple women (5 to be exact) hasn't helped his reputation much either.

Catherine Zeta Jones

Catherine Zeta Jones is an Academy Award winner and a triple threat. She can dance, sing, and act all at the same time but following her public confession of mental health issues and how she struggles with bipolar disorder, Hollywood producers have discretely chosen to not cast her anymore. The real reason is that she is uninsurable, and without cast insurance, a film can't me made. The prejudice against mental health is a major dilemma in the film industry and according to the actress herself, it's not the only reason she's kept from the good roles these days.

Robert Pattinson

Pattinson struggles with depression issues and has a hard time finding work due to his personal problems. His *Twilight* days should have resulted in a long-term career. It doesn't help that his ex-girlfriend, Kristin Stewart, and former co-star embarrassed him in the press with her unexpected affair with director Rupert Sanders.

Mike Myers

Myers is actually super controlling behind the scenes, making filming with him harder than it looks. Myers is known to those in Hollywood as a total perfectionist who doesn't let anything go by without his approval on it. Cast and crew of his films know that he is hard to handle, which is why after his hit *Austin Powers* films his roles were mostly voice over ones.

Shia LaBeouf

Shia is rude without him being on set and he is very hard to work with on set as well. Shia is a method actor, meaning he becomes his character in order to prepare for the role. As such, Shia takes on the traits of his character and it can be rather unpleasant. The situation came to a head while Shia was filming the movie *Fury* alongside Brad Pitt, who said Shia disappointed him with his behavior.

Edward Norton

Norton is the nightmare of most directors. He isn't being considered for roles because no one wants to work with him.

Russell Crowe

Russell Crowe is known for his temper. Crowe, talking about his film *Gladiator,* was quoted as saying, "It was shit, but I'm the greatest actor in the world and I can make even shit sound good." Crowe also has a sense of entitlement so high, and his ego eventually ended up getting the better of him, and he slowly got less and less offers, as directors didn't want to work with him.

Madonna

Industry workers don't like Madonna's behavior on the set of her films and her inability to listen to the director. There is a reason why her films aren't as good as audiences thought they would be. She didn't like taking cues from anyone, even when it would have benefited her greatly.

Sean Young

Sean Young, now deceased, was almost fired entirely from the 1987 movie *Wall Street* by director Oliver Stone. Young acted like a pure monster on set, terrorizing the cast and crew and making it extremely difficult for others to work on the film. It's amazing how actors forget who they are and how to work when fame goes to their heads. My daughter was the costume designer on a film that had Young in it several years ago, and she reports that Sean made impossible demands not only of her department, but all the creative people on the set.

Mel Gibson

Between the racist and anti-Semitic remarks to his diva-like behavior behind the scenes, Mel Gibson quickly became persona non grata with the film and television industry. Gibson was said to have a serious temper problem and would go on rants that would make everyone feel downright scared to be around him. Gibson was a great actor and director, but he is a disturbed individual in real life.

Cybill Shepherd

Cybill Shepherd has not been seen in anything for quite some time – for a good reason. Shepherd was a complete and utter diva on the set of her sitcom *Cybill*, so much so that a character was created on CSI to mimic her behavior. That character ended up being a murder victim. Writers, directors and producers are well known for killing off characters in their stories. A relevant story was that of *"Rat Patrol,"* a Mirisch-Rich TV series that became a hit. The actors demanded major raises to continue their roles for the second season. Producer Lee Rich responded that it was a war story – that all the actors could be killed anytime he wanted – and their roles would be re-cast. That shut them up.

Christian Bale

Christian Bale has a damaged reputation for his misbehavior on the set. During the filming of *Terminator Salvation*, Bale was caught on tape yelling at the director of photography, "You are trashing my scene. You do it one more time and I ain't walking on this set if you're still hired. You're a nice guy. But that don't cut it." Bale later apologized, and a good thing, too. Behind the scenes, in the entertainment industry, employees have been known to sabotage an actor's work, leading to an actor's being laughed out of the industry.

There's a joke that illustrates that: An actor is is playing a role in a Shakespeare play, and so badly, he's booed and heckled from the audience, which he ignores. Then, a tomato is thrown from the audience and hits him. He responds, "I didn't write this shit, you know."

Sharon Stone

Sharon Stone's success got to her head and she became more and more selective about the roles she decided to take after *Total Recall, Basic Instinct,* and *Casino.* She had a 'manager,' Chuck Binder, to whom she was devoted for over 30 years, and they made decisions together, so it may not have been all her fault, but it got to a point that Stone was so selective that offers just stopped coming in. She parted ways with Binder just last year, but by then, it was probably too late.

Gwyneth Paltrow

Gwyneth's offer to star in films have dried up recently due to the fact that she isn't fun to work with. Besides, she is in to her personal website, Goop, and that may be taking too much of her time. Also, she defended Harvey Weinstein, who is today's villain for sex abuse in Hollywood, which rebounded on her. On the set of *Iron Man 2,* Paltrow was "not friendly to anyone, and tends to make people feel awkward and uncomfortable. She wasn't outright rude to Scarlett Johansson, she just didn't ever speak to her. Gwyneth went out of her way to avoid Scarlett." Sometimes actors forget to be professional.

Chevy Chase

Chevy Chase is one of the hardest people to work with, which is why his career is no longer. Chase once referred to Cary Grant, one of the most revered film stars, on Johnny Carson's show, as a 'nance,' which got him barred from the show. Chevy got his start on *Saturday Night Live* and Chevy began to display inappropriate behavior and anger issues. Chase slapped Chery Oteri during a rehearsal and angered Will Ferrell, who went to Lorne Michaels, the executive director and creator of SNL to complain. Chase was banned from SNL from that day forward. Chase's anger problems still exist – I read in the Los Angeles Times recently that Chase was in a road rage incident and caught up with the guy who cut him off – and was beaten up.

Lindsay Lohan

Lindsay no longer acts, due to the fact that she was so hard to work with when she was hired for a film that after a while it was not worth it. Lohan began to get a reputation of being a pain to work with on the set of the film *Georgia Rule* alongside Jane Fonda. Lohan was constantly late to set and when she did come she had a hard time remembering her lines and keeping it together. James Deen, the porn actor, and her co-star on the film *Canyons*, called Lohan a "child lashing out." And she has been seen in a hijab, a Muslim shroud that women wear, leading some to speculate that she has become a Muslim.

Kiefer Sutherland

Sutherland was the star of the television show *24*. His co-star on the show, Freddie Prinze Jr., said that Sutherland would come to set drunk sometimes and would proceed to go to his trailer and sleep it off, stopping the production until he was able to work. Behavior like that is not tolerated, inexcusable and unprofessional. Other actors and below-the-line workers hate it when they can't get home to their families at a reasonable hour.

Katherine Heigl

Katherine Heigl is notorious for being one of the most difficult people to work with in Hollywood, both in television and film. Heigl has been said to be very demanding on set, cold to the other members of the cast and crew and even snobby with fans who line the streets to see her when she makes an appearance. Heigl also has a very unwise tendency to talk badly about former films and shows she has been on, thinking it won't come back to get her. Well, it did as Heigl isn't acting very much these days.

Josh Duhamel

There are those who say that he is a very temperamental behind the scenes of his films and has a serious jealous streak with his wife, Fergie. Duhamel is said to be very controlling of Fergie when he thinks no one is looking and is very aggressive when on set as well.

Jennifer Lopez

Jennifer Lopez is known as a diva to her musical co-workers, but her behind the scene film behavior is no different. Lopez comes to productions with a long list of demands that have to be fulfilled by the time she gets on set or else she becomes an increasingly impossible person to work with. Plus, she is known as a snob. That could be why Lopez's roles began drying up fairly quickly.

WHATEVER HAPPENED TO HOLLYWOOD "CLASS?"

Hollywood has always cast itself as a "class act," above the fray, upstanding when it comes to triumphing over the wrongs perpetrated against society – think *"Mr. Smith Goes to Washington;"* or celebrating the triumph of faith over the pursuit of filthy money – think *"It's a Wonderful Life;"* and/or the triumph of sheer courage over adversity, in *"The Stratton Story."* Hey, come to think of it, all these movies starred Jimmy Stewart, my former client as a publicist.

In *those* days, and I know how this sounds, the spectacle of real movie stars campaigning for Oscars was so far-fetched as to seem mythical. Never did one see full page ads in Variety or the Hollywood Reporter, paid for by Stewart, Spencer Tracy, Clark Gable, or others, demanding, or as is the case these days, pleading to be rewarded for their work on film. Yeah, guys rule – they always did, but neither did you see Bette Davis, or Ingrid Bergman, or even Betty Hutton begging for attention.

So what has happened to "class?" "Crass" is what happened to "Class!"

Movies once meant something – they galvanized us during both world wars, and even played a part in uniting us during the Korean War. Not so much in the Vietnam years – until *"Deer Hunter"* came out some years later. Mike Cimino directed – he was a veteran of commercials. It made us look at Vietnam with new eyes. Then success of that film led to the making of the most expensive flop at that time, *"Heaven's Gate,"* after which Cimino disappeared. Cimino, last I heard transitioned into a woman. I guess he was really affected by making that movie.

Movies made us laugh when laughing was the furthest thing from our minds – and best of all – they told stories - real stories.

We looked up to movie stars – they seemed bigger than life – Hell, they *were* bigger than life. They made a lot of money, compared to us, and their lives were glamorous. At least the parts they let us see. Movies became our statement to the rest of the world. Other countries made movies too, but no one seemed to care, not even in their *own* countries. American movies helped make us the most envied country on earth – everyone who wasn't here wanted to be, and they came, in waves. And what happened? *Today* happened.

Starting in the early 1960s, movies became *real*. TV had happened, and the third generation of moguls, who were mainly agents and lawyers, thought that the old glamour didn't sell anymore. Out with Doris Day and Rock Hudson. In with Peter Fonda and Dennis Hopper. I never saw Cary Grant go into a bathroom, much less shut the door behind him. Today, if an actress doesn't pull down her panties and squat on a toilet, why bother to see it? And "frowing up," ...don't get me started. When did Jimmy Cagney, or Loretta Young upchuck on film? Never, that's when. Every film made today, so it seems, has the now usual and regular vomiting scene.

Call me old-fashioned. I am. I like real stories, about real people, winning over real adversity and overcoming real problems.

The Oscar show, which everyone in the world, it seems, used to watch, has been dropping in popularity for years – each year the audience dwindles. It's a commentary on how little Hollywood films mean today. This year, it's even bleaker, and I expect even less people will want to watch.

The ten (used to be five) nominated for "Best" have been seen by more people who got free screeners from the Academy than who actually went and paid to sit in a theatre.

Who approved making *"Mother?"* Stand up – show your face, take your licks. Why was that a good idea? $13 million worldwide? Didn't pay for the advertising. Yeah, I know all about how Jennifer Lawrence and director Darren Aronofsky "did it" together. Proof that an actress and her director should be 'hands off' during production. Think of Ingrid Bergman and Roberto Rossellini. Bergman, a big star in Hollywood, wasn't taken seriously after that. Perhaps that should have been a warning.

"Captain Fantastic"? Only $15 million? Must be all Viggo Mortensen's relatives lining up at the boxoffice.

And *"Manchester by the Sea,"* a 'popular' picture if ever there was one. Casey Affleck is accused of being a sex abuser, and it's obvious why he wanted to play that part (hint: to win an Oscar). A slew of Oscars and nominations, but only did $77 million, worldwide. And to the accountants, who really run the studios these, it's a loser.

And $46 million for *"Ladybird,"* up to now. Although the recipient of many honors, I'm certain that in the fabled bowels of the Hollywood hit machine, a mysterious cabal of executives jumped up in unison, shouting "This is a home run - don't let this one get away"!

TV ads compete and cannibalize each other. For all the time and money drowning the campaigning for Oscar, the box-office returns this year are a big yawn. Given how expensive TV and print ads are, I would think this is close to the last year of the traditional Oscar campaign.

So, are we doomed? That great Hollywood wit, Robert Downey Jr., said that he thinks the bigger studio movies are where quality is starting to happen. As that great lamented stick figure of the 60s, "Mr. Bill", would say, "Oh Nooooooooooooo...

So, *Batman* and *Spiderman*, *Ironman*, and *Superman* are our future. No wonder I watch Turner Classic Movies, instead to going to movie theatres.

Russians in America

Sexual harassment of actresses in Russia is the same as in Hollywood, but no one talks about it because they are terrified they will be made to "disappear." I read about Xenia, a young actress who had a job interview with a director 40 years older. She was in her second year at Moscow's theatrical university. "He closed the door and told me to take off all my clothes," Xenia said. "I asked him what for, and he immediately kicked me out, grumpily yelling that he had no interest in actresses who ask questions instead of doing what they were told to do."

Anna Pukhova, a Moscow-based actress, has had similar experiences. She lost out on two gigs after turning down "intimate offers," the Daily Beast reported. "All my life, since school, I've heard that the bed opens doors in theater, but I refused to believe that such a disgraceful thing could be true," said Pukhova, now a theater director. "There is always a chance to say 'No' – but at the cost of losing a job or other opportunity," she said.

A unique event occurred in my life at the office one day in 1959. The U.S. and the Soviet Union were at war – the Cold War, and I remember clearly how, just a few years earlier, in school, we were trained to hide under our desks to escape impending nuclear holocaust. The Russkis were our enemies; we heard it from everyone from President Eisenhower to Walter Cronkite. Imagine my surprise one day when Mr. Skouras told me our two countries had decided, as an attempt to lessen the building threat of war, on a cultural exchange. Russia was sending a showbiz contingent, although I doubt they would have put it that way, to America and we would dispatch a like product there. Since no one else wanted to deal with the hated foe, or had refused to, I, as a low-ranking but well-dressed corporate apparatchik was designated to greet and spend a lot of time with three Russian film people.

I went to the airport with Murray, our staff photographer and met the then-president of the Russian Film Academy, gray-haired and imperious Ivan Pyryev, their version of Marlon Brando, tall, blonde and handsome Yuri Yakovlev, and Russia's answer to Katherine Hepburn, Julia Borisova. They were attended by a large group of large men who, I was told, were "interpreters." I didn't know what an interpreter was supposed to look like, but even at my tender age, I didn't think they were that. Also, the three guests spoke no English and therefore I could communicate with them solely through one of the large men. Or, in Julia's case, a large woman.

Pyryev had directed a new film version of Dostoyevsky's acclaimed literary masterpiece, *"The Idiot,"* which starred Yakovlev and Borisova, and we had decided to send them Rona Jaffe's *"The Best of Everything,"* starring an assortment of young Fox contractees like Barry Coe, Hope Lange, the model of the moment, Suzy Parker, and with a cameo by Joan Crawford. Oddly enough, when I met Rona to do some PR with her, pre-release, I found out that her father, Dr. Samuel Jaffe, had been principal of P.S. 139, my public school, in Queens. She and I had been in the same classes and didn't know each other until then.

The Russians were installed at the Waldorf-Astoria and I accompanied them on a sightseeing trip around the city. The six-hour circumnavigation of Manhattan Island is to be avoided, if possible. Especially in cold weather, and if one is subject to seasickness. We did the Radio City Music Hall, the Cloisters, the usual museums, and even a jazz joint in the Village, something they especially wanted to do. We ate three meals daily together for three or four days before departing for Boston, thence to Philadelphia, where I left them as they boarded the train for Washington, D.C., where Fox's political machinery was to take over.

They were excited and wide-eyed to be in America, and I was fascinated by their clothes, their appearance, Julia's beauty, and their ability to drink copious amounts of Russian vodka without seeming to get drunk. I later found out their vodka was a mere 40 proof, compared to our 80 or even 100 proof. That was, and I guess still is, their secret.

We learned to communicate rather well through facial expressions, hand gestures, and my drawing pictures of things or pointing and naming them, with the Russians supplying their words for it. I became especially close to Yuri, the young actor and, after several days, satisfied we couldn't actually speak to each other, the interpreters left us pretty much alone. Late one night, the both of us absorbing most of a bottle of vodka, I began to suspect that perhaps his lack of English was a tiny bit overstated. In an unguarded moment, I shot Yuri a question in English – and he answered it. He was terrified and begged me not to reveal what had just happened. It would be curtains for him (my expression, not his). The interpreters were, of course, KGB, and all three of my new friends could understand and speak English, however in a limited way. At different time, Julia and Yuri both told me of intimidation and sexual harassment they had to endure to participate in the Russian film industry. It was exactly the same as in Hollywood. They were to pick up whatever they could in the way of intelligence, not military, but opinions about themselves and their country, and to learn from our citizens what they could about our intentions.

I would like to say I was proud of my fellow Americans during the time I traveled with my Russian friends, but because we were told they didn't understand our language, some pretty crude and unflattering comments were made about them, sometimes right in front of them, that embarrassed and even shamed me, especially after I found out they understood every word. Or almost every word. Some of our slang got past them and I was grateful for that.

When we said goodbye, they plied me with presents, a half dozen bottles of vodka, several cartons of Russian cigarettes, and two exquisite lacquered boxes, which I still have. Mr. Pyryev also startled me by, after insisting we take a photo together, which I also still have, inviting me to come to Russia, where he would install me in the Russian film school and make me a director. Imagine that. That was just around the time that Van Cliburn won the Tchaikovsky competition in Moscow and made the cover of Time magazine as a symbol of a breakthrough. Had I accepted Pyryev's offer, that might have been me on that cover. He also told me something else – we had been discoursing in English by then – he predicted that in the future, not in his lifetime, but perhaps in mine, we, Russians and Americans, Caucasians both, would naturally be allies in a global war against the brown-skinned people.

Men Want Sex

Oh, is that a surprise? The male brain is programmed to seek sex over food, a study in the publication Nature, says. Cole Porter wrote, *"Birds do it, Bees do it, even educated fleas do it."* Scientists at University College London find that all male animals would do anything to get it. Everybody knows about Praying Mantises – the male sacrifices himself, the female eats him while he's doing it. That's extreme – I don't know any man or boy who would go that far. But neurons fire up in the male brains of nematode worms, and researchers say that it is likely that similar mechanisms are at work in humans. Female nematode worms don't have the same neurons. Apparently, sex for females comes after edibles. Is this proof that male and female brains are wired differently? I say yes. And so would every man and woman I know.

We make adrenaline in our own bodies. It's the basis of the 'flight or flight" mechanism – which instantly tells us in a moment of extreme danger whether to fight the threat, or run – if we have the time. Adrenaline is addictive – hence 'adrenalin junkies," those who constantly seek danger out – riding on the most extreme rollercoasters, or flying a jet plane. Adrenaline is compared to morphine in addiction terms. Or men, or women, who get an adrenaline rush when they cheat. Withdrawal compares to Frank Sinatra's acting in *"Man With the Golden Arm"* – horrible and frightening. Which is why so few 'come down' off the high.

Cheating, however, is something that men do less well. I always got caught. My theory is that women make the best detectives. They always seem to know. Honesty doesn't work, either. If I told either of my wives that I wanted to have sex outside, they'd leave me. And they did.

I did cheat, however, in marriages and long-term relationships. It wasn't the sex itself, it was the lying that got me into trouble. Lying is quite the vogue today – after all, our president does it and he seems to get away with it. In fact, the more he lies, the more popular he is with his base.

Monogamy, in my opinion, doesn't work. Men are programmed to impregnate every female that comes by his cave. Women want to improve the genes of their unborn child, so they seek the best-looking, healthy male, who seems a good provider. So they cheat, too. At least they should. They should also make the same money as men.

Monogamy is artificial, something that religion dreamed up. Ditching a marriage, ruining their kids' lives over something like sex doesn't help anyone.

I often thought maybe the trick is to have multiple marriages, say, every five years. Nah, women want children, and the alimony and child support would be a killer.

In today's times, pre-marital sex is okay with most millennials, as is porn, for both boys and girls, courtesy of the Internet. I talk to high schoolers – the kids of my friends, and what they're doing I could only dream about when I was a teenager. I find them both sophisticated and bored with sex. On the other hand, I read that kids today are not doing it because they're holed up in their room, on social media – sexting. Also, open relationships are quite the thing nowadays.

I read recently that Americans are having fewer babies and less sex than ever before, way below replacement rates. I understand that other cultures, too, are avoiding sex. The Japanese are in crisis, because children are not experimenting like they used to. In fact, because of the low birth rate, women wanting to have a career, and the rapidly aging society, that the last Japanese will die in 2800. *The last Japanese!*

Russia is prompting their citizens to have more children. And they're paying, or at least offering tax breaks, as is Germany. Western countries produce less children than deaths. Some economists predict that over the next 50 years, European countries will be Muslim majority, because they have outsize families.

I've found, as I get older, that sex isn't as thrilling as it once was. Of course, I've had addiction problems with it, as I wrote in my previous book, *All is Vanity.* The men that I hang with all say that marriage destroys sex, and they didn't enjoy sex after a couple of years. Especially once their wives had a baby. There must be something to that urban myth of the Madonna-whore complex. Maybe the fact their wives are mothers, mean that men see their own mothers, and as we know, there's a built-in inhibition about incest.

Women Have Needs, Too

Yes, men cheat – the figure I read is 75% - but women cheat too, at least 50% of them do. Women in their 40s are having great sex, and not with their husbands.

As porn on the Internet increases, viewership among females is growing. Female infidelity is virtually guaranteed to pass male cheating – there are more women than men on this planet. From personal research, I've found the most common age for women to have an affair is 45. For men, it's 55, which bears out in my *personal* survey.

Cheating is not a sign of an unhappy marriage. Women cheat because they are unhappy with their relationship, or loneliness, for revenge against their husbands cheating. They get more upset by the emotional aspect of cheating rather than the physical side, because of the rejection of their bodies, or them. Men cheat for sexual variety, or at least that's what I've heard from men.

Women Are Predisposed by Genetics to Cheat

Women are predisposed by their genetics to have affairs as "back-up plans," if their relationships fail, according scientists at the University of Texas, who say humans are not naturally monogamous. The team's research, in a white paper, has described the "mate-switching-hypothesis" which says humans have evolved to keep testing their relationships and looking for better long-term options. The senior author of the research, Dr David Buss, told the Sunday Times: "Lifelong monogamy does not characterize the primary mating patterns of humans. Breaking up with one partner and mating with another may more accurately characterize the common, perhaps the primary, mating strategy of humans." For our distant ancestors – when disease, poor diet and minimal healthcare meant that few people lived past 30, looking for a more suitable partner was necessary. "A regular mate may cheat, defect, die, or decline in mate value. "Ancestral women lacking a back-up mate would have suffered a lapse in protection, and resources."

Some Wives Allow Husbands to Cheat

Did Hilary Clinton have an agreement with Bill that allowed him to cheat on their marriage once a year? Or twice a year? Or always? Some people think so. Does this qualify as an 'open' marriage? Jane Ridley, reporter for the New York Post, writes about 'infidelity' clauses in marriages. Masha Lopatova, wife of former NBA player Andrei Kirilenko, says that she sets the 6-foot-9 Russian-born athlete "free" once a year. Linda Jones, wife of Welsh singer Tom Jones,' put up with his famous, talked-about philandering for 59 years. Open marriages are popular in Europe - in America, it's usually a case of "don't ask, don't tell," where the wife ignores the man's sex life outside the marriage. Another option, as psychotherapist Joe Kort asserts, is the "eyes wide open" approach that involves a written contract full of rules. "For example, the woman might agree that the man can attend BDSM play parties once a month or have oral sex — not penetrative sex — once a week, so long as he has blood tests every three months," says Kort, of Detroit, who often advises clients in mixed-orientation marriage — with one straight spouse and one who's gay.

Bill Clinton

For years I specialized in married women. These women told me they were cheating not to wreck a marriage, but improve it. I was amazed when some told me they had an agreement with their husbands that they didn't talk about their affairs. They had children, businesses, assets in common, and decided that splitting up would only cause pain for the kids, and would reward their lawyers. They told me they found married life incredibly dull and resented the fact they felt they had to work harder than men to support it.

I have never used rubbers – in fact – I would turn down women who insisted on it, because I knew I was healthy, and because I didn't feel the intimacy. 'Try eating candy without unwrapping it... That's what a condom is like', says Rodrigo Duterte, President of the Philippines.
Some Catholic women, and others who believed in the rhythm method, would have sex with me on their non-fertile days of the month, having 'maintenance sex' with their husbands on the others.

And they are everywhere. I've been picked up in the produce department of supermarkets, on city streets, while driving, in the normal course of business, or, believe it or not, by referral.

Married women, in my opinion, are the best lovers. They are anxious to please, because they've been in long-term arrangements where sex has become a sometime thing, and they're certain they've lost their appeal – but they're wonderfully grateful, and it's a good feeling to know you've helped them in concrete ways. Arrogant? Supercilious? I don't agree.

I'm a pretty good cook, so lunchtimes were always ideal. One has to eat, yes? I'd make a light but nutritious and creative meal, with a suitable wine, following which we'd explore each other's passions for a couple of hours. I'd hear all about their lives, and why marriage was so difficult, how in-laws sucked, children were ungrateful, husbands only interested in business and sports, how their illusions about life had vanished, and their youth and beauty were gone.

I, however, was delighted to remind them that their looks, their bodies, their passion, their sexuality, and their ability to please a man, were all intact. Here was the proof. And then they'd leave.

I've often heard from them that their marriages improved, that they'd become more loving not only to their husbands, but to their children, as well. There were many women, but not once did I hear from any of them that they wanted to leave their situations for me. Nor did I ever want them to. They had their homes, their positions in their communities, their charge accounts, soccer games, hair and nail appointments, and SUVs. And I was glad of it.

After 20 years or so with the same partner, sex can and does become boring. Sex with someone new is exciting, as it was in the distant past, until morality and religion made it 'forbidden'. Sex provides a dopamine rush similar to a drug-induced high. Try it – you'll like it. Until you get caught, that is.

Sex Addiction

Sex addiction was defined officially in a study done by the University of California, Los Angeles, in 2012. Since then, a University of Cambridge study found that one in 25 millennials are now addicted to sex - a number that is rising because of the Internet porn industry. To be addicted to sex is a problem, and requires treatment. It wrecks marriages, and destroys careers. I know, because I had it. Sex, it was explained to me by a string of psychoprofessionals, was a form of self-medication.

The Society for the Advancement of Sexual Health, an education and sex-addiction treatment organization, estimates that between 3 and 5 percent of the U.S. population—or more than 9 million people—could meet the criteria for addiction. Some 1,500 sex therapists treating compulsive behavior are practicing today, up from fewer than 100 a decade ago, say several researchers and clinicians, while dozens of rehabilitation centers now advertise treatment programs, up from just five or six in the same period. The demographics are changing, too. "Where it used to be 40- to 50-year-old men seeking treatment, now there are more females, adolescents, and senior citizens," says Tami VerHelst, vice president of the International Institute for Trauma and Addiction Professionals.

Women have been my obsession and my profession all my life. Unable to ever please my overbearing and emotionally and physically violent mother, I devoted my youth and most of my adulthood to pleasing any woman I could. I dated them, married them, represented them, hired and fired them, and, in general admired them. And still do. I know a lot about what constitutes beautiful women and their behavior. After all, I was at various times, in a position to raise the status in Hollywood of any number of beautiful young women. So completely fixated was I, that I developed a nasty case of Satyriasis, which if you didn't know, is male nymphomania. Another popular name for it is sexual addiction.

There were times I was seeing as many as seven women at once. I thought then that was a glamorous version of me. But each wanted to be with me on Saturday night, or on my birthday, or on Christmas. You get the picture. Where was I when I wasn't with them, they wanted to know? I created much anger because the lies I was telling were too difficult to keep track of. I always got caught eventually, and any Freudian will assure you I wanted to be caught. Perhaps I did. But it didn't stop me, no more than a gambler can stop gambling, or an overeater can pass a Krispy Kreme stand, without serious intervention.

I thought I had graced the edge of Nirvana one afternoon, when I hosted a table of four, myself and three women at the Polo Lounge of the Beverly Hills Hotel, to celebrate the conclusion of a successful fund-raising for a major Los Angeles charity. Two of the women were married, and the other wasn't. Under the table, feet were moving. I was almost delirious. I was turned on, like all power-hungry men, by knowing each of their secrets, and having control over so many women at the same time.

The orgy circuit I occasionally traveled in the '70s was as much social and business as it was about sex. The Greenfield manse in Rancho Mirage, although populated by swingers, also was, by his invitation only, open to male casting directors, producers, directors, and actors and actresses. On occasion, a female film worker who liked the action was also invited. This tended to bring him closer to the people he did business with, or wanted to draw nearer into his agency operation. After all, once you've shared certain intimacies with people, you've formed an affinity group. Although no pictures were taken (that I know of), obvious secrets were manifested, which could be kept – or not.

Encounters which involved group sex in Paris, Madrid, Mexico City, Acapulco, and Cuernavaca, a wealthy vacation town some fifty miles from Mexico City favored by the Jet Set, were both business and social, in that I was in those cities on business, and the people I met at grand homes were rich and occasionally famous. Sometimes these events, which would go on for several days, would lead to lucrative contracts, or financing for entertainment projects. If one were affable, polite, and educated, one invitation would lead to another. I found then, as an American, that, unlike today, we were looked up to and admired.

Some medical doctors or psychiatrists will tell you that mania can't be created by environment, but must be located in a faulty gene structure. Not true, at least in my case, because after many years of destructive behavior that cost me marriages, relationships, jobs, and a great deal of pain, I took serious action to beat my problem. Over the years, I had psychological counseling from psychiatrists, and psychologists, including a former nun. I thought she, as a woman, might have some special insight. But what would a nun know about a man's sexual nightmares? She might know about her own.

I learned a few things during hypnosis, from a professional hypnotherapist, a woman I was dating, who said she could cure me. But right after the session we would immediately have sex.

I even tried a 12-step program fashioned on the successful Alcoholics Anonymous model, but devoted to my particular addiction. *"Sexaholics Anonymous"* was a lot of fun. Did I get anything out of it? I got laid - a lot. Imagine a group of sex addicts, at least half of them attractive women who can't say no, and you see what was for me, Toyland. I sold it to myself as "research" for the script I was writing. The program was located in Hollywood. Imagine locating a sex addicts group in Hollywood. What were they thinking?

I was told I could examine my devils better by writing about my feelings, keeping a journal of my thoughts, desires, and how I coped with them. But having been around creative people all my life, naturally I wrote a screenplay about a guy who has everything he's ever wanted, who throws it all away – over and over – for a quick orgasm. Sound familiar? Many powerfully seen men have the same problem, and it's linked to the same kind of childhood I had. Former president, Bill Clinton, comes to mind. The most powerful man in the universe risks being fired and denigrated in the history books forever for a furtive, half-completed blow job behind a door in the Oval Office? You couldn't write that into a movie and get away with it. But of course it happened. And I know at least a half dozen other guys I've met over the years, in *and* out of the business, with the same problem.

Was it dangerous? Very. But that doesn't faze addicts. After all, what's another drop of water to a drowning man? Diseases were always a possibility, but probably because of a strong immune system, I never got any. Outraged husbands or boyfriends were something to look out for, but except for the time an LAPD motorcycle cop almost pulled his gun on me, I always got away with it.

A recent not-so-funny story about a friend of mine, David Stein: A few minutes past midnight he is cruising the Internet, accessing one of several of the dating services he is registered on, which has an instant message feature, when to his surprise, a woman pops on and says "Hi." He answers back and 5 minutes of email banter later, he invites her to call him. A several-minute conversation leads to an in invitation and believe it or not, of all the places in the Universe she could be, she lives ten minutes away from him. Fancy that.

Twenty minutes later he is at her door with a bottle of champagne, and ten minutes after that, they are in bed. David acquits himself well and is feeling grand on his way home at 2:45 a.m., when two Newport Beach cops pull him over, saying he was crossing the white line. Cops always pull motorists over in slack time with a weak excuse just to toss the car and its inhabitants to see what they can find. Sometimes they say it's a broken taillight, or they couldn't see the license renewal tag. It's usually bogus because their sergeant will want to know what they were doing between midnight and 6 a.m. if they haven't got a caseload.

While one cop administered a roadside DUI test, the other got to work seeing what he could find. He ignored the two joints in David's ashtray because it's merely a $100 citation for under an ounce, but sparked to the large wrench with the taped handle peeking out from under David's front seat. "Ah Ha," he said, "A deadly weapon." Out come the handcuffs and David's on his way to the slammer, while his car is towed to the impound.

David is in the rag business and drives around the worst parts of downtown at all hours and kept the wrench in case he ever needed it. No matter. He is photographed, fingerprinted, outfitted in orange jumpsuit pajamas and safely locked away. Bail is $4,000. Next morning, given a yellow pages, David locates a bail bondsman who springs him. The same yellow pages produce a law firm who will gladly take the case. So, ten grand later, David is free and able to concentrate on the message here, which is: One minute David is getting laid. Next minute, David's in jail. How perfect. How expensive. And how dangerous. The woman could have been a psycho; she could have been a lure for a robbery. Anything's possible. But for a sex addict, no logic or reason applies.

I finally controlled my addiction through Yoga and meditation. After I left my marriage to Linda Jones, I moved into a penthouse apartment in Beverly Hills, determined to rein in my impulses because it was costing me the things I most wanted

Female Sex Addicts

I've known sex addicts of both sexes. In my travels I met several women who couldn't get enough - the guys were lined up. I remember one incident when I was walking into an apartment building to meet a friend for dinner, when I heard a woman call to me from an upper floor. I looked up and saw this young woman, who gestured to me that she had unlocked the door, and that she was on the 8th floor. Thinking she might have a medical emergency, I went up in the elevator and as I got off, I could see her, dressed in a robe, standing in her open door of her apartment. I entered – and was attacked. She was naked under the robe, and I was in my 'what-the-hell' days anyway. I might have been anybody, as much as she cared. We did it – and I left – slightly lighter, and only five minutes late for dinner. Never saw her again, although I looked. She must have moved.

My mother was always on me to meet women with whom she was either friends with, or knew their mothers, who had unmarried, or divorced daughters. And they were anxious to meet straight, unattached men – which, in Los Angeles, are exceedingly rare. I was always loath to meet her choices, mostly because she had terrible taste. I did meet a couple of them, and the dates were always awful. Except for the one who was the daughter of a producer-writer whom I admired. He was a star,

responsible for some of the best comedy shows on TV or on Broadway. I said yes, and called on his daughter – who was a divorcee. Same thing happened as before. Within five minutes, after a glass of white wine was poured, we had our clothes off and were active on the living room rug. There seemed no reason to go out for dinner, so we said goodbye, and I left. Again, never saw her after. Too embarrassed, I guess.
I even saw, through my friend Phil Marshak, who directed adult films, an Italian porn flick that had one female tasking on 1,000 guys over a weekend. They'd "come and go."

'I think about sex *all* the time'. Rose Bretécher suffered with sexual thoughts for years, a form of Obsessive Compulsive Disorder. From her first vision of a naked boy aged 15, until she underwent therapy to overcome the hallucinations and anxieties that left her unable to live normally. In her book, *Pure*, Bretécher reveals that the more she tried to rid herself of the images, the more likely it was they would appear. She told ES Magazine, that despite desperately trying to live a normal teenage life, anti-depressants made the problem worse.

The most effective therapy has been Exposure and Response Prevention (ERP), which involves the sufferer directly viewing the images that haunt them. Of the therapy, she said: 'I was exposed to sexual content of gradually increasing explicitness and encouraged to tolerate my anxiety, thoughts and feelings, without engaging in compulsions

Fritz Was A Fucker

I represented the irrepressible and immensely talented animator and filmmaker, Ralph Bakshi, right after he completed "*Fritz, the Cat*," the X-rated feature-length cartoon in 1972. It caused a commotion both in Hollywood and across the U.S. You have no idea of the fuss kicked up by "*Fritz*" in the media. Imagine cartoon animals screwing right up there on the silver screen, twenty feet high. And "high" is the operative word, since it became a cult favorite to see it while stoned. The film made tons of money, and a star out of Ralph.

Brains of Sex Addicts

HealthDay reporter Robert Preidt wrote that in people with sex addiction, pornography affects the brain in ways that are similar to that seen in drug addicts as they consume drugs.

"There are clear differences in brain activity between patients who have compulsive sexual behavior and healthy volunteers. These differences mirror those of drug addicts," study author Dr. Valerie Voon, of the University of Cambridge in England, said in a university news release. The study was published in the journal *PLoS One*.

"The patients in our trial were all people who had substantial difficulties controlling their sexual behavior and this was having significant consequences for them, affecting their lives and relationships," Voon explained.

"In many ways, they show similarities in their behavior to patients with drug addictions," she said. "We wanted to see if these similarities were reflected in brain activity, too." The study participants' brain activity was monitored while they watched either pornographic videos or sports videos. While watching the pornographic videos, the men with sex addiction showed much greater activity in three areas of the brain compared with men in the control group.

According to the researchers, prior studies have suggested that sex addiction -- an obsession with sexual thoughts, feelings or behavior that they are unable to control -- affects as many as one in 25 adults.

Sex For Sale

Young people are selling their bodies online to pay student loans, make the rent, or afford designer labels. It's true in Japan, South Korea, the UK and in America, too. Nancy Jo Sales, writing for Vanity Fair, says, *"The girlfriend experience"* is the term young women in the sex trade use for a service involving more than just sex. "They want the perfect girlfriend, and I charge $700 an hour," says Miranda, 22. "Almost all of my friends do some sort of sex work . . .. It's almost trendy to say you do it—or that you would."

Seeking Arrangement, Seeking Millionaire and Date Billionaire, are just several of the Web sites which match "sugar daddies" with "sugar babies," whose company the daddies pay for with "allowances."

'I guess I could just start 'camming,' or doing sexual performances in front of a Webcam for money on sites like Chaturbate" says one interviewee. "It's not like you need a pimp anymore. You just need a computer. If anyone tells you they're not sleeping with these guys, they're lying, even if it's just a blow job, because no one pays for all that without expecting something in return."

"Basically every gay dude I know is on Seeking Arrangement," says Christopher, 23, a Los Angeles film editor. "And there are so many rent boys," or young gay men who find sex-work opportunities on sites like RentBoy.

Gayness

Half of us have 'gay genes' and if you have a big family, the greater the chance of having a homosexual son, a study claims. Genes influence orientation. It's an evolutionary predicament because gay men have almost no offspring to which they pass on their genes. Therefore, half of us must have 'gay genes' for homosexuality to remain. Giorgi Chaladze, of the Ilia State University in Georgia, published the article in Springer's journal Archives of Sexual Behaviour.

Jason Koebler, writing in U.S. News & Reports, writes that scientists may have finally solved the puzzle of what makes a person gay, and how it is passed from parents to their children. Scientists suggested that homosexuals get that trait from their opposite-sex parents: A lesbian will almost always get the trait from her father, while a gay man will get the trait from his mother.

The hereditary link of homosexuality has long been established, but scientists knew it was not a strictly genetic link, because there are many pairs of identical twins who have differing sexualities. Scientists from the National Institute for Mathematical and Biological Synthesis say homosexuality seems to have an epigenetic, not a genetic link.

Long thought to have some sort of hereditary link, a group of scientists suggested Tuesday that homosexuality is linked to epi-marks — extra layers of information that control how certain genes are expressed. These epi-marks are usually, but not always, "erased" between generations. In homosexuals, these epi-marks aren't erased — they're passed from father-to-daughter or mother-to-son, explains William Rice, an evolutionary biologist at the University of California Santa Barbara and lead author of the study.

Evolutionarily speaking, if homosexuality was solely a genetic trait, scientists would expect the trait to eventually disappear because homosexuals wouldn't be expected to reproduce. But because these epi-marks provide an evolutionary advantage for the parents of homosexuals: They protect fathers of homosexuals from underexposure to testosterone and mothers of homosexuals from overexposure to testosterone while they are in gestation.

"These epi-marks protect fathers and mothers from excess or underexposure to testosterone — when they carry over to opposite-sex offspring, it can cause the masculinization of females or the feminization of males," Rice says, which can lead to a child becoming gay. Rice notes that these markers are "highly variable" and that only strong epi-marks will result in a homosexual offspring.

"Most mainstream biologists have shied away from studying it because of the social stigma," he says. "There are many examples of homosexuality in nature, it's very common."

I've read recently that homosexual behavior is also produced by chemicals in food and drinking water that predispose males and females to same sex attraction. Frogs and fish have been found with intersexual organs in response to estrogen that is flushed into municipal water supplies that current filters are no defense against.

Non-homosexual male might sometimes show interest in homosexual behaviour without having a homosexual identity. In flocks of sheep, up to 8% of the males prefer other males even when fertile females are around. In 1994, neuroscientists found that these males had slightly different brains to the rest. A part of their brain called the hypothalamus, which is known to control the release of sex hormones, was smaller in the homosexual males than in the heterosexual males.

The neuroscientist Simon LeVay in 1991, described *a similar difference in brain structure between gay and straight men.*

Sex Addict, Porn Addict

Democratic Congressman Anthony Weiner pleaded guilty to a felony involving sexting messages to a 15-year-old girl. He said he couldn't help himself, even though it threatened his marriage, his relationship with his son, and his job.

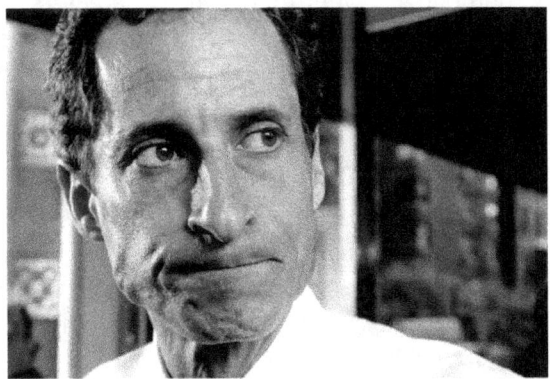

Photo Richard Drew AP

A new report confirms sex addiction and addiction to pornography are real disorders that have serious consequences. "There is no debate about the reality that there are people who struggle with sexual behavior disorders," said John Giugliano, past president of the Society for the Advancement of Sexual Health, in article for "Mental Health Month." "Most recent neuroscience research examining addiction-related brain changes in Internet pornography users points to substantial evidence of such changes." Experts say that streaming pornography is addictive.

The report is SASH's recommendation to the committees of the American Psychiatric Association's Diagnostic and Statistical Manual of Mental Disorders and the World Health Organization's International Classification of Diseases.

Gayness in Films

Gay characters were played by actors, straight and homosexual, in films such as *Call Her Savage*, the first film to show homosexuals, *Our Betters*, *Footlight Parade*, *Only Yesterday*, *Sailor's Luck*, and *Cavalcade*. Gay male characters were dandyish, bumbling, even decadent characters. Franklin Pangborn, one of my favorites, is always portrayed as a hotel manager, or front desk guy, who is *always* embarrassed and frustrated by the ridiculous circumstances he finds himself in. Edward Everett Horton is another.

Marlene Dietrich, whom I represented at the Arthur Jacobs company, and was bisexual, started a trend when she began wearing men's suits, in the 1930s. She caused consternation at the premiere of *The Sign of the Cross* in formal dress, with top hat and cane. If you saw a film that Bob Fosse directed, either *"All That Jazz,"*
a thinly disguised story about himself, or *"Cabaret,"* you saw female dancers in various states dressed as men. Liza Minnelli, also appeared in men's clothes.

Gayness in Animals

Are 'gay' animals employed as actor's in Hollywood movies. Of course they are. "Lassie" was a guy playing a girl. And nobody has said that King Kong wasn't a guy – or was he?

The birds and the bees are gay, according to the world's first museum exhibition about homosexuality among animals. With documentation of gay or lesbian behavior among giraffes, penguins, parrots, beetles, whales and dozens of other creatures, the Oslo Natural History Museum concludes human homosexuality cannot be viewed as "unnatural."

"We may have opinions on a lot of things, but one thing is clear -- homosexuality is found throughout the animal kingdom, it is not against nature," an exhibit statement said. Geir Soeli, the project leader of the exhibition entitled "Against Nature," told Reuters: "Homosexuality has been observed for more than 1,500 animal species, and is well documented for 500 of them." "The sexual urge is strong in all animals. ... It's a part of life, it's fun to have sex," Soeli said of the reasons for homosexuality or bisexuality among animals.

One photograph shows two giant erect penises above the water as two male right whales rub together. Another shows a male giraffe mounting another for sex, another describes homosexuality among beetles. Bonobos, a type of chimpanzee, have sex with either males or females, as part of social bonding. "Bonobos are bisexuals, all of them," Soeli said.

Gay penguins have adopted an abandoned chick - and the wildlife park claims they are the 'best parents' it's ever had. Two male Humboldt penguins were given the egg, which hatched in April. The egg was laid by a female called Isobel, who had to abandon it to find food. Each time Isobel lays an egg, her partner Hurricane refuses to sit on it. It is the second egg the males have adopted after the first failed to hatch. The one-month-old unnamed male chick is said to be doing 'really well'

Domestic rams are statistically among the mammals most likely to form gay relationships, with 8 per cent of male sheep forming male-to-male bonds. Dolphin males have also been known to pair up, with relationships lasting as long as 17 years. Homosexual wild Australian black swans sometimes form threesomes with two males and a female, which has led to higher breeding successes.

Female gorillas have been spotted engaging in same-sex behavior. Australian scientist Dr Cyril Grueter made the discovery while in Rwanda. Of 22 gorillas observed across two years, 18 engaged in same-sex activity. 'They were obviously deriving sexual pleasure from each other. 'Gorillas are closely linked to humans and we thought by looking, we could learn a little more about our own evolution.' Over a quarter of the homosexual events that Dr Grueter observed included at least one female that had been involved in sex with a male the day before or after.

Male fruit flies, in their first 30 minutes of life, they will try to copulate with any other fly, male or female. I know some guys like that.

Male king penguins Stan and Olli were dropped from the Berlin Zoo breeding program after keepers noticed they only had sex with each other, and moved them in with another gay couple, Juan and Carlos in the Hamburg Zoo.

Two male lions were spotted 'mating' in Botswana safari park after ignoring other lionesses'. Lawyer Nicole Cambré, who took the pictures during a safari trip, Biologists have recorded same-sex sexual activity in more than 450 species including emus, chickens, koalas, salmon, cats, owls and dolphins, flamingos, bison, beetles and warthogs. Alaskan Albatrosses also pair up male and male and female and female.

Zoologist Petter Bockman, an expert on the subject at the University of Oslo, says: 'If you ask: "Can animals be gay?" The short answer is: "Yes." "Gay" is a human word, however, so we prefer to use the word "homosexual" for animals. One Pentecostal minister told him he would 'burn in hell' for his work. Funnily enough, another said the money would be better spent 'curing gay animals'.

During the winter mating season, competition is fierce for access to female Japanese macaques. Males don't just have to compete with other males for access to females: they have to compete with females too. That's because in some populations,

homosexual behavior among females is not only common, it's the norm. One female will mount another, then stimulate her genitals by rubbing them against the other female, says Paul Vasey of the University of Lethbridge in Alberta, Canada, who has been studying these macaques for over 20 years.
I saw on the Internet recently, a male macaque attempting to have sex with a male deer. The deer was OK with it.

On the other hand, zoologist Lucy Cooke, in her new book, *The Unexpected Truth About Animals: A Menagerie Of The Misunderstood,* says that Giant Pandas have sex 40 times in an afternoon. I would try that, but I'd be hard-pressed to find a woman to do it with. The Adelie penguin female uses payment in kind – she'll have sex with any bachelor as long as they pay up with pebbles to build up her nest. I know some women like that. Male penguins with have sex with anything that moves, including dead penguins. I know some guys like that.

Gayness is extremely common across the animal kingdom, from insects to mammals. **Many humans are homosexual, so, is it natural?**

Before You Have Sex With Animals

Sex with animals causes penile cancer. It could be a matter of life or death, according to a new study finding that men who had sex with animals were twice as likely to develop cancer of the penis as others.

The study of 492 men from rural Brazil found that 35 percent of study participants, who ranged from 18 to 80 years old and included both penile cancer patients and healthy men, reported having sex with animals in their lifetimes. A team of urologists from centers around Brazil co-authored the paper, which looked at risk factors for penile cancer in men who had visited 16 urology and oncology centers in 12 Brazilian cities.

Men who had sex with animals also reported a higher incidence of disease. Of the 118 penile cancer patients, 45 percent reported having sex with animals, compared with 32 percent of healthy men, who visited the medical centers for benign conditions. Fifty-nine percent of men who had sex with animals did so for one to five years, while 21 percent continued the behavior, also known as zoophilia, for more than five years. The subjects reported a variety of frequencies for their sex acts, ranging from monthly to daily.

The researchers found no association between penile cancer and the number of animals the men used over time, the species, which included mares, cows, pigs and chickens, among other animals, or the number of other men who also participated. However, the higher rate of reported sexually transmitted diseases in men who had sex with animals could be a result of group sex, said lead author Stênio de Cássio Zequi, a urologist in São Paulo. More than 30 percent of subjects practiced sex with animals in groups.

Currently, 30 U.S. states, under their animal cruelty legislation, have enacted laws that prohibit sexual contact between humans and animals, according to Michigan State University College of Law.

Sex with animals could be as ancient as sex itself. The study is the first to link the practice to male genital cancers. Penile cancer accounts for up to 10 percent of cancers in men in Asia, Africa and South America, although it is rare in the U.S.

Micro-injuries to the penis are a well-recognized risk factor for the development of penile cancer. Such physical trauma could explain how sex with animals causes the cancer.

"We think that the intense and long-term SWA practice could produce micro-traumas in the human penile tissue," Zequi said. "The genital mucus membranes of animals could have different characteristics from human genitalia, and the animals' secretions are probably different from human fluids. Perhaps animal tissues are less soft than ours, and non-human secretions would be toxic for us," he explained.

Köhler, who specializes in sexual medicine, speculates that the friction during SWA causes micro-lesions. "The vagina in humans has moisturizing properties, which prevent penile injury. With animals, you're at higher risk for micro-trauma, like cuts and scratches. And then whatever pathogens are there, like bacteria and viruses, are more likely to cause a problem."

Circumcision also seems to play an important role in the development of penile cancer in men who have sex with animals. In global populations where the foreskin is removed soon after birth, the rates of penile malignancies are near zero. Uncircumcised men may develop more micro-traumas during sex, according to one theory on why circumcision protects against cancer. Smegma, the white secretion that collects around the glans of the penis in uncircumcised men, is composed of fatty acids that have been shown to be highly carcinogenic, and could also help to explain the increased risk.

The subjects recruited from the study all grew up in rural areas of Brazil. The researchers wrote that they chose this population to investigate because sex with animals is common in rural areas with high rates of penile cancer, and a connection seemed plausible. In fact, Zequi said he was not surprised that 35 percent of participants had had sex with animals.

"We know that in rural zones of our country, and probably worldwide, young men have sexual experiences with domestic animals," he said. Most of the subjects reported that they stopped having sex with animals when they began having sex with people.

"SWA is not a sexual behavior limited only for poor rural populations," Zequi said. "It is actually a growing health concern today. Just give a few clicks on the search sites on the Internet and you'll come across numerous 'zoo' sites or virtual communities focused on bestiality, many of which are pornographic and sometimes with degrading images." Zequi wants men (and women) who have sex with animals to know that the practice could be hazardous to their health, and he wants clinicians to spread the word to at-risk populations.

Köhler agreed, saying, "From a penile cancer prevention point of view, SWA should be discouraged based on the results of this study." He recommended standard safety precautions with any type of high-risk sexual intercourse: Wear a condom. The new study was published online Oct. 24 in the Journal of Sexual Medicine.

Don't Have Sex While sleeping – Or Do

'Sexsomnia' sufferers have sex in their sleep, and don't remember it. Sleep disorders include walking, talking and even eating without realizing it. And now, sex. CBS2's Dave Carlin reported patients are now being diagnosed with "sexsomnia." They go through a sleep study where doctors chart and prove they are truly asleep while engaging in sex acts — alone or with others. The patients have no recollection of it afterwards. "If your partner is sleeping and they're not aware of it, that's not OK," one woman said. Sexsomnia is rare, and doctors say more men than women have it. Of course.

Dr. Saul Rothenberg is a sleep specialist with Northwell Health. He said sexsomnia falls in the same category of parasomnias as sleepwalking and sleeptalking.

"Normally, you're either asleep or awake and in parasomnias, including sex, you would have an incomplete awakening,"

Rothenberg explained, "so you're stuck in sleep, but you start doing things that are normally restricted to waking."

Sexsomnia was used as a defense in two high-profile rape cases overseas, and the juries in those cases bought the argument.

The cases were a man in England in 2007 who was acquitted of raping a girl, and a man in Denmark in 2013 who was acquitted of molesting two girls.

"I never heard of it," said Joe Watson of Garden City, Long Island. "Sounds pretty shocking to me if that held up in court." Rape victim advocates worry more criminals will try to use it as a defense. Meanwhile, researchers say for those who really have sexsomnia, there is no known cure. They suggest minimizing or avoiding these potential triggers – stress, sleep deprivation, sleeping pills, and excessive alcohol and drug use.

A Swedish man who was convicted of rape had his charges overturned after an appeals court found the man could have been asleep during the attack and cited "sexomnia" as a reason he should be released. Mikael Halvarsson was acquitted of rape this month after experts said he was asleep during the attack and had no memory of the incident, according to a translated court ruling from the Sundsvall appeals court in Sweden.

Halvarsson was accused after the victim woke up as Halvarsson allegedly assaulted her on April 2, 2014. They had been sleeping in the same bed, but they each had their own blanket, according to the translated court documents, which also noted that she called the police the next morning, and they found Halvarsson still asleep in her bed when they arrived.

In the appeal, Halvarsson's previous girlfriend testified that he had previously tried once to have sex with her when she was sleeping. When she stopped him, he then acted confused and asked what had happened. His mother also confirmed that he had disturbed sleeping patterns before. While the term sexomnia may seem made up for the purposes of getting away with a crime, Dr. Kingman Strohl, a professor of medicine and director of research at the Sleep Center at Case Medical Center in Cleveland, confirmed it's an actual medical diagnosis that includes unintentional sexual behaviors during sleep.

When Women Lose Men

Dr. Craig Morris, an evolutionary biologist at Binghamton University in New York, says that, 'Our thesis is that the woman who "loses" her mate to another woman will go through a period of post-relationship grief and betrayal, but come out of the experience with higher mating intelligence that allows her to better detect cues in future mates that may indicate low mate value,' said Dr. Morris. Hence, in the long-term, she "wins". The "other woman", conversely, is now in a relationship with a partner who has a demonstrated history of deception and, likely, infidelity."

What Everyone Gets paid For Porn

I always wanted to know what actors get paid for sex in front of the cameras. My friend Phil Marshak told me what actors and actresses get in porn films, and what he got as a director. Phil offered me the opportunity to take part in one of his films in a category called "geezer porn," in which I would have to perform with either one or two young girls – and get paid for it. I considered it - and demurred. And then again, in the past, actors were thought of as a low class profession, along with prostitutes. Remember: an actor shot Lincoln.

Chris Morris, a reporter for CNBC, reports the facts.

A superstar performer, with name recognition that extends beyond adult entertainment, earns more than a newcomer, and is based on the sex act. The average actress' compensation is between $800 and $1,000. Stars can earn as much as $1,500 to $2,000, while newcomers with bad representation might earn as little as $300. Anal shots get higher rates - $1,800 to $2,500.

Talent
Female performer, man/woman scene
Female performer, all-woman scene
Male Performer
Director
Cameraperson
Sound Technician
Production Assistant
Writers
Still photographers
Makeup artists

Men receive a fixed rate per scene or day, averaging $500-$600 per scene or day. Male stars earn $700-$900, superstars up to $1,500. Writers earn less - $250-$400 per day. Camerapersons, can earn $500-$700 per day. Sound technicians get $300 and $400 per day. Production assistants pick up $100 to $250.

My sister was a graduate of the filmmaking school at UCLA, and her first job was in the porn industry, working as a makeup person for a co-graduate, who was building a rep as a director. She got to cover up pimples on the asses of men and women, add "glisten" to the labia of actresses, and lug equipment around the shoot. She was paid $500 for working a full day on set.

The Future: VR porn

Naughty America, one of the U.S.'s largest pornography production companies, produces Virtual Reality porn. Naughty America only has around two-dozen VR porn videos for its subscribers to experience. Ian Paul, the company's chief information officer, told me they're producing one to two new VR porn videos every week, but as more users become more interested in VR porn, Naughty America will ramp up production accordingly to meet demand. I look forward to trying it.

Use It or Lose It.

My urologist, the late Dr. Cliff Marshall, insisted I have at least four orgasms a week – he didn't care how I achieved it. He said, "If you don't want to have prostate, or testicular cancer, you have to clean out your scrotum regularly." That was many years ago, and I haven't had cancer of the lower regions…yet.

I did read research from Harvard University, published in the journal European Urology, July of 2017, which said that ejaculating at least 21 times a month (that's five times a week for those of you who can't count), significantly reduces a man's risk of prostate cancer. Cliff knew that 20 years ago.

I also saw that researchers at the University of Montreal, published in Cancer Epidemiology, men who have sex with multiple women are almost a third less prone to develop the disease, reducing their risk of prostate cancer by 28 per cent. Celibacy doubles the risk of the disease. I use that as an excuse.

"Don't knock masturbation. It's sex with someone I love." -- Woody Allen.

Some parents scared their adolescent children by telling them, "You'll go blind," or 'Your palm will grow hair." Remember those?

Woody Allen

Masturbation kills up to 100 Germans a year, according to a study which has also uncovered the bizarre ways people have died. One man - wearing pantyhose, a raincoat and a diving suit as well as a plastic bag over his head - died in Hamburg after sitting next to a heater and trying to melt slices of cheese on his body.

Another man in Halle was found dead with Christmas tree lights clamped to his nipples having apparently tried to stimulate himself by electrocution.

Forensic examiner Harald Vow said the most common reason for autoerotic deaths was the desire for the ultimate orgasm through depriving oneself of oxygen.

Between 80 and 100 people across the country accidentally die every year due to risky masturbation practices, his study found. In one example, a man was found suffocated in the cellar of his home in Hesse having apparently tied chains around his body and neck.

Masturbation relieves tension and stress by flooding the system with endorphins, which are the body's natural feel good chemicals, and helps with insomnia, as Mel Gibson said to his then-wife, Oksana, when he couldn't sleep, 'at least a blow job." After all, he was paying for it. Oksana refused, which led to a punch-up. The cops were called...and you remember the rest.

You're Never Too Old

Frequent sexual activity can boost brainpower in older adults, says a study from Coventry University and Oxford. Researchers found that people who engaged in more regular sexual activity scored higher on tests that measured their verbal fluency and their ability to visually perceive objects and the spaces between them.

The study, published in *The Journals of Gerontology, Series B: Psychological and Social Sciences*, involved 73 people aged between 50 and 83. They didn't ask me – probably were warned off.

However, Herbert Johnson, 92, of Stuart, Florida, has been ordered to stay out of Martin County public libraries after coming on to female employees. A Martin County deputy visited Johnson at home, handing him a trespass warning for all county libraries. If Johnson isn't careful, assault with a dead weapon could be next.

80-year old Jane Fonda is still doing it – at least she says she is still doing it.

What Some People Might Call Weird Sex

- Humans are the only animals that anal fuck. Did you ever wonder why?
- Humans are the only animals that fuck face to face.

BDSM

Stephanie Pappas, LiveScience Senior Writer, says that BDSM practitioners are healthier than 'Vanilla' People. Their sexual preferences are listed in the fifth edition of the Diagnostic and Statistical Manual of Mental Disorders as potentially problematic, but people who play with whips and chains in the bedroom may actually be more psychologically healthy than those who don't.

A new study finds that practitioners of *bondage, discipline, sadism and masochism,* or BDSM, score better on a variety of personality and psychological measures than "vanilla" people who don't engage in unusual sex acts. BDSM is a sexual practice that revolves around those four fetishes. The study was published in the Journal of Sexual Medicine.

A Swedish Doctor's Back Door Policy

A Swedish doctor has been shown the back door following his curious use of massages to treat common medical conditions, such as headaches and back pain. Sweden's Medical Board of Responsibility revoked the medical license of "Doctor Anal" after years of warning him about his unconventional treatments. The doc claimed to have attained "very good results" with the massages, according to The Local, a newspaper. He was warned for performing the unorthodox method when he performed the technique on an elderly woman. She described the procedure as "an incredibly offensive encroachment." And Sweden's medical board called it "dubious for a number of reasons" including that the muscles that actually needed to be relaxed couldn't be reached. He gave an interview to Aftonbladet, a Swedish tabloid, explaining his unique bedside manner to being on the autism spectrum.

Have a Tiny Dick? Don't Buy a Ferrari

Urologists have come up with a technique for surgically correcting micropenis, a condition in which the penis makes a short stop. Men who suffer from micropenis are unable to have sex or to pee standing up. Phalloplasty involves taking skin from the forearm and shaping it into a four- to five-inch penis, with the original glans transplanted to create feeling.

Cosmetics For Sex?

I owned a cosmetics company a couple of years ago, for about 15 minutes – it was called LeDerma, and the two partners, one a dermatologist, were cashing out. They had turned the business over to me because I had the knowledge and contacts to make it a public company by backing into a 'shell,' a public company that wasn't trading. Long story, but it didn't happen. On the way, I got some education about the cosmetics business and what goes into it. More later.

However, baby foreskin, apparently, is the way to a smooth, younger-looking complexion. The anti-aging business is a billion dollar industry, and both men and women will try anything to get a youthful face or body. HydraFacialMD, treatment claims to be highly effective at improving overall skin health and remedying fine lines and wrinkles, skin texture and advanced signs of aging.

Dr. Gail Naughton, who developed the technology, told NY Magazine, "As we age, our cells divide at a slower rate, which contribute to the telltale signs of aging, like wrinkles and loss of firmness and luminosity. Growth factors captured from the donated foreskin of a baby are at their peak ability in promoting rapid cell turnover. Applied topically, they spur adult skin cells to regenerate. This is said to have a smoothing effect on the skin."

Tom Cruise swears that a smearing of bird-shit on his face is all he needs to stay young. According to Now magazine, Cruise has told friends that his skin has never looked better thanks to the expensive spa treatment, which involves mixing feces from a nightingale with rice bran and water, which is then applied as a facemask.

Redheads

The three redheaded girlfriends I've had were excitable, fast to get angry, and hid out from the sun. I thought they were very passionate, and quick to go to bed. Colin Fernandez, writing in MailOnline, says scientists claim they have found genes that show hair color was a risk-taking personality and affects how likely someone is to have sex. Natural redheads – both men and women - delay having sex until an older age than people of different hair coloring. I've always favored blondes.

Men Fake Orgasms Too

I've never done it, but some men claim they're faking it.. Women can make the right sounds at the right time to convince their lover they're having an orgasm when they're not. But for men it's a little more difficult to hide, and while vaginal sex was the most common place to fake it, men also reported faking orgasm during oral sex, anal sex and manual stimulation. I don't know how they do it. *It should* be obvious.

The Military's Problem

The military has problems with preventing sexual assault, writes Charles Dharapak, for the AP. I assume it is because the army and especially the Marines, are taught that violence wins, and that macho men get all the girls. I know several ex-marines, and in my own family, an army member who says their training was at fault. Female police and deputy sheriffs I've met and spoken to on ride-alongs have to exceed the men in being hard, if they are to be taken seriously.

Jake & his Floating Balls

I was told this story by Jake, a sometimes friend. He comes home very late one night – He's been out catting around, and he's drunk. His wife is waiting, with a gun in her hand. She's a former biker girl and tough as nails. He really thinks she is going to shoot him. She demands he remove his pants.

"Ah ha," he thinks to himself –"luckily, I showered – no pussy smell."

She then orders him to "Get on your knees!" He's terrified as she walks around behind him – he thinks she's gonna shoot him in the back of his head.
"No, please, you don't wanna do this….you don't understand, I can explain…I was in a traffic jam on the 405, I really was…people got hurt, I was trapped."

"Yeah, we'll see. Get your ass up and fetch a pan of warm water."

Scared, and confused, he does it. She says: "Back on your knees!" He quickly complies.

"Drop your balls in the water," she barks!

Wha?

"Do it!" she says, and cocks the hammer – And he does.

And they sink. "OK, you can get up now."

Relieved, he stands up; she puts the gun down, and embraces him.

"What was that all about," he asks, his heart pounding.

"If your balls had floated," she replies, "I would have killed you, because I would have known you had come in some other pussy, and where I 'm from, you would now be dead!"

And luckily, he was too drunk to come.

5 Things a Man's Finger Length Says About Him

Is your index finger shorter than your ring finger? Tanya Lewis, Staff Writer, Live Science reports: A smaller 2D: 4D ratio has been linked to a longer stretched penis size, according to a 2011 study published in the Journal of Andrology. While the men were anesthetized, researchers measured the lengths of the men's fingers and penises, both flaccid and stretched. The shorter the index finger relative to the ring finger, the longer the stretched penis was.

Men with short index fingers and long ring fingers are nicer toward women, according to a new study, published in the journal Personality and Individual Differences. The more testosterone, the longer the ring finger grows.

Men who have a shorter index finger than ring finger may also have more handsome faces, suggests a study published in the journal Proceedings of the Royal Society B. The amount of testosterone a baby is exposed to before birth can affect how the individual's face develops, and how attractive that face is, the researchers said.

A 2010 study published in the British Journal of Cancer, said that men whose index fingers were the same length or longer than their ring fingers were 33 percent less likely to be diagnosed with prostate cancer during the study than men whose index fingers were shorter.

Polygamy increases risk of heart disease

Dr. Amin Daoulah, a cardiologist at the King Faisal Specialist Hospital and Research Centre in Jeddah, Saudi Arabia, says the risk and severity of heart disease increased with the number of wives. In the Muslim religion, if you can afford it, you can have four wives. I could have told him that, and I'm not a doctor. Of course it does – having one wife, one at a time – is stressful. But times four? It's got to be hell. The HBO series, *Big Love,* starring Bill Paxton, with Jeanne Tripplehorn, Chloe Sevigny and Ginnifer Goodwin as the wives, eventually led to the death of Paxton. That was fiction, but I can imagine it as fact.

Dr. Daoulah said: "We found an association between an increasing number of wives and the severity and number of coronary blockages. This could be because the need to provide and maintain separate households multiplies the financial burden and emotional expense. Each household must be treated fairly and equally, and it seems likely that the stress of doing that for several spouses and possibly several families of children is considerable."

Have 'period shame'?

Easy, a Canadian company, that has a delivery service of organic tampons, has taken a new direction away from the usual ads for period products, with powerful ads that show women with a tampon string hanging out or bleeding during a bath.

Clemence Michallon, writing in Dailymail.com, says that the ads include changing a blood-stained sheet, bleeding during a bath, or using a hot water bottle for pain relief, and undressing for a swim, in which a woman is shown with the string of her tampon, which can be seen hanging out of her body

'We wanted to do something that made people talk about periods because it's something that is still looked at as taboo or shameful, which is a bit ridiculous in this day and age,' CEO Alyssa Bertram, told Marketing in a previous interview. 'By addressing it and talking about it, it reduces that shame and that stigma.'

Ass Augmentation Using Implants

An article in *Plastic and Reconstructive Surgery®*, the official medical journal of the American Society of Plastic Surgeons (ASPS), says that butt augmentation is one of the fastest-growing forms of plastic surgery for women. I can't imagine it being for men. Fernando Serra, MD, and colleagues of Pedro Ernesto University Hospital, Rio de Janeiro, Brazil, says that women undergoing placement of silicone implants to improve the shape of the buttocks are very popular in Brazil because of the "Miss Bum Bum" contest, which celebrates women having the most acreage in their caboose.

Teens & Risky Sex

A 2011 national survey conducted by the Centers for Disease Control and Prevention showed that 47 percent of high school students had had sexual intercourse, and 40 percent of those who were currently sexually active did not use a condom when they last had sex. I was sexually active in high school, when those figures were much lower, and we couldn't buy 'rubbers,' as they were called then. We were too embarrassed to ask the pharmacists, and they wouldn't sell it to us anyway. Then a solution occurred to me; I got a job as a soda jerk at Doc Gordon's pharmacy, on Queen's Blvd, and 63rd Road, in Forest Hills, New York, when I was 15. Before I was fired – for putting too much tuna on sandwiches – Doc was very cheap – I managed to squirrel out rubbers to my friends when the Doc took cigarette breaks.

Having Erection Problems?

Bernie Sanders, who some Americans would say would have made a better president than the incumbent, says that relationship with one's mother determines the quality of an erection. In an article published in Psychosomatic Medicine, he said that cancer was linked to psychological well-being, and that factors which could cause it included unresolved hostility towards your mother, hiding aggression behind 'a facade of pleasantness - and not enough sex. 'Sexual adjustment seemed to be very poor in those with cancer of the cervix,' Sanders wrote, quoting the journal.

Olivia Foster, for Mailonline, reports that Sanders could be right, that problems with erectile dysfunction could be directly related to how good a relationship a man has with his mother. The study published in the Journal of Sexual Medicine, shows that having a strained relationship with your mother as a boy can lead to sexual issues as an adult. The survey was conducted by the Charles University in Prague.

Robot Brothel

A robot brothel could soon open in the UK to allow men to perform 'any of their sexual fantasies', reports Shivali Best For Mailonline. Lumidolls opened its first robot brothel in Barcelona earlier this year. The realistic dolls will allow people to legally fulfill any fantasy. The good news: A robot brothel could also wipe out the risk of STIs in the sex industry.

Sex at Dawn

A couple of evolutionary psychologists David M. Buss and David P. Schmitt, published a book about human sexual behavior in prehistory called "Sex at Dawn."

I can attest to it. And so can most men. I remember Roger Moore, in one James Bond movie, says, "I'm an early riser."

Have a Threesome

I've referred to group sex before, when it was called "swinging" in the 60's and 70's, or until AIDS came along and stopped it. but there's now an app for threesomes - 3nder — pronounced "Thrinder" – rhymes with "Tinder." New York is 3nder's second-biggest market behind Los Angeles, and it's popular with millennials. A 27-year-old art student and 3nder user, Melissa, tells Jane Ridley, interviewing her for Discovery, about her wild ride on the app, which connects both singles and couples looking for group sex. For five months, I was a 3nder "unicorn" — an unattached female. We're called unicorns because we're pretty rare.

Just like Tinder, you log on via Facebook and are presented with pictures and profiles of people in your area. You swipe right if you're interested, or to the left if you're not. Then you can exchange texts and phone numbers. It's an easy way to find both couples and singles."

Labia as Jewelry

Tracy Kiss uses her own labia as jewelry. Ginny Weasley, in Health magazine, reports that Tracy, who lives in London, in an interview with Metro, explains how her gynecologist analyzed a blister due to the excess skin on her labia and she elected to have it removed. After the operation, Tracy kept the skin. "I had distending labia, and after keeping it in a jar, it turned from pink to dark." In a video on her blog, Tracy goes into how she made two wrinkly, slug-like bits of her own skin into a glittery pendant. Is this too much information? She dried them out, applied pink paint and sparkles, and used gem tar to make a choker. "Its substance may not be quickly clear to the clueless eye or to everyone's taste" says Tracy, "yet that is its magnificence." She has attained notoriety for her adoration for *sperm smoothies* and semen facials.

Speaking of Labia

Writer Allison Ramirez had a perfume made up blending her vaginal juices and essential oils. She claims men are turned on by it and even a cashier in McDonald's being 'a little nicer to me than normal'. Claudia Tanner, reporting from Mailonline, quoting Ramirez, says it WORKS! The Los Angles journalist, writing for Cosmopolitan, tested it out on dates - one man kissed her excitedly and said: 'I can't help it. It's that scent you have.' The scent we give off – chemicals known as pheromones – are believed to play a big role in attraction.

After carrying out some research into how, writer Allison Ramirez discovered 'you basically just have to stick a finger down there and then use the finger to dab your "natural perfume" on your pulse points.' According to the history books, this was a method of seduction used by courtesans of medieval Europe, who spritzed their vaginal secretions behind their ears and necks and on their chests. One romantic encounter ended with a smooch in a photo booth and another led to a text to meet up again. Pheromones are chemicals that are secreted in our sweat and other bodily fluids that are believed to influence the behavior of the opposite sex, such as triggering sexual interest.

Lots of experiments prove men find women far more attractive and attainable when ovulating than at other time of the month.

A team at the University of Texas, Austin discovered that men judge the smell of a T-shirt worn by the woman during fertile phase as more pleasant and sexy than a T-shirt worn by the same woman during her non-fertile phase. Researchers said ovulating women release a signaling chemical, a type of pheromone called a copulin, which could prove a boon for perfume manufacturers. Dating firm Pheromone

140

Parties organizes events to match people by their smells and last year Smell Dating became the first 'mail odor dating service' using three-day old T-shirt samples.

The Los Angles journalist, who carried as part of an experiment for a Cosmopolitan feature, consulted with Saskia Wilson-Brown, the founder and director of the Institute for Art and Olfaction, who runs perfume-making workshops. She told her that essential oils rose, cinnamon, aniseed, and benzoin have aphrodisiac qualities and could work mixed with her womanly juices. However, she warned that 'body fluids and sweat are not stable, and probably wouldn't do well in a formula'.

Saskia also informed her scents like pumpkin pie, lavender, licorice, and *doughnuts* have been found to increase blood flow to a man's erection in a study carried out by the Smell and Taste Treatment and Research Foundation in Chicago.

In the end, Allison settled on creating a sweet-smelling scent of her vagina secretions mixed with cedar, rose and civette. Armed with her 'secret weapon', Allison then tested out her new perfume by going out on dates. On the first night, she met up with an old friend and ended up sharing a drunken kiss with him in a photo booth. 'Then all of a sudden, teeth!' she wrote. 'It was funny, but it also kind of hurt.' She says he replied: 'I can't help it.

Allison added: 'The rest of the night was a blur, but his comment and actions were a pretty good indicator that my perfume was working.' Days later, Allison wore her scent for a date with a friend of a friend. She revealed he didn't say or do anything during the date to indicate the perfume had worked but he did text her later saying he had fun and asking her out again.

A leading gynecologist has hit out at men who complain about the natural smell of their partner's genitals, which she describes as a 'form of abuse'. Dr. Jen Gunter, who is also a prominent critic of Gwyneth Paltrow's controversial Goop website, revealed she once dumped a boyfriend for complaining about the smell of her genitals. Writing in her blog newsletter, the Canadian expert urged women not to feel ashamed and feel they have to resort to buying harmful products that create artificial odors. She says they upset the vagina's natural pH balance and leave you at a greater risk of infections like gonorrhea and even HIV. She wrote: 'If you think you have a medical condition, see a doctor. If your partner insinuates that an artificial smell is preferable to the smell of a normal vagina they are the one who has an issue.

Women are to Blame

Blame women for the increase and, um...'depth' in sexy movies. *Variety* says women make up more than 60 percent of the moviegoing audience, and they are also voracious readers of tabloids, such as *The Globe,* or *National Enquirer,* which are sold in the checkout lines of supermarkets. They are also the audience for sexy books like *"50 Shades of Grey,"* and the three movies made from that best seller. I haven't read the book, nor seen any of the films. But nearly every woman I know has.

Did you know that Sperm navigate by using musical tricks?

Similar to a guitar string, sperm beat their tail with two different frequencies or "notes". Scientists from the research center caesar in Bonn, associated with the Max Planck Society, and the Helmholtz research center Jülich published these findings in an article in Nature Communications.

The sperm tail serves multiple purposes: it is used as a propeller that drives sperm forward, as an antenna that captures and processes sensory stimuli, and as a "rudder" that sets the course accordingly. Sperm swim forward by waving their tail. As the wave travels from the head down to the tip of the tail, liquid is pushed backwards and sperm are propelled forward. For steering, the tail beats asymmetrically to one side, acting like the rudder of a boat; consequently, sperm move on a curved path.

The new study shows that sperm use a surprising mechanism to produce an asymmetric beat. Two different waves travel along the tail: one with a fundamental frequency and another with twice this frequency. To put it in musical terms, sperm play notes of different octaves. The tail undulates more to one side compared to the other. This time-modulated wave provides the essential feature for steering: liquid is pushed asymmetrically, but in contrast to the rudder of a boat, the symmetry is broken in time rather than in space. The study also shows that, when sperm sense the female hormone progesterone, the frequency, amplitude, and phase of the two waves is adjusted and thereby also the swimming path. Thus like fine-tuned instruments, sperm play chords orchestrated by the chemical signals encountered while cruising along their path.

Gun and Sex Violence in Films

In 1972, I addressed a group of high schoolers during Hugh O'Brian's seminars for youth, the Hugh O'Brian Youth Leadership Foundation. Hugh O'Brien was the star of several TV series, including *"Wyatt Earp."* He asked me to talk about the incredible violence and sex acts being portrayed in films at that time. When I was growing up, I saw every movie I could, and violence then, was off-camera. You saw an actor firing a gun. Some years later, you saw actors fall down. But you never saw blood. You never saw the film stars of the 30's and 40's making love. Kissing was OK, but as I've said before, closed mouths – and 5-8 seconds long.

Here's the speech I made:

Opening remarks by MICHAEL SELSMAN at the Hugh O'Brian Youth Foundation Seminar, May 29, 1987 at Pepperdine University.

"Good evening: I've been influencing your thoughts since you were born! And so have the others on this panel, and everyone else who does what we do for a living. For most of my professional life, I have manipulated the media to present the views of companies and people I've represented, as well as my own. In public relations, I've spoken for organizations that produced oil, toys, leisure time activities, films and TV, hotels, advertising agencies and personalities. As an agent, I've represented well-known directors, actors, writers, producers and literary works. And I have produced movies and TV shows. And what have I learned?

That I have the ability via the media, to influence the thinking of people worldwide, both living and yet unborn! Pretty powerful stuff, in my opinion, and which is why I was glad to be asked here tonight. The subject is "Reel Power," and thanks again to the media, we know what that means: Big Bucks! And all it buys...Ok, I'm all for living well, and you'll hear a lot about power and how to get it and how to hang on to it. But I want to focus tonight not on the advantages of power, but the responsibilities of power.

We who shape public opinion are more culpable for the state of mind of the public than any other group of product pushers. And what are we pushing these days? You already know the answer: Drugs, sex and violence! Close your eyes for a moment and try to imagine a world without television. Yes, there was such a time. TV didn't exist until I was almost your age. I grew up reading. You grew up watching.

As a group, humans relied on visual images for millions of years before we had language. We are eyes-oriented. I'm not concerned, as some educators are that kids don't read anymore. Why should they? Kids today are smarter than they've ever been! Because of the cosmic video explosion, TV has become the dominant social force in our lives. It brought down McCarthy, Nixon and Johnson and helped end the Vietnam War. It also gave us the Moon landings, the African famine, Ronald Reagan and Jim and Tammy Bakker. We can now see instantly and with startling clarity the best and worst instincts of humankind.

My concern is our apparent celebration of the lowest tendencies of our species as portrayed in films and on TV. Tomorrow morning, as an experiment, sit down in front of your TV and watch systematic mind conditioning of the very young. Watch how empty minds are trained to respond to problems in communication with violent action! Not with compromise and negotiation. And those are their heroes! Is it any surprise we adults have worshipped the mafia, as portrayed in "The Godfather," Gordon Liddy of Watergate fame, and now Col. Ollie North, the "true American Hero"? Stick around for prime time and watch the carnage; the guns, the killing, the half-dressed women luring men to their destruction. Interrupted cunningly with commercials for all kinds of alcohol and drugs for headaches to hemorrhoids, and everything in-between.

TV has become a habit, perhaps the greatest drug of all. And like all drugs, it's addictive. In America, the average household has their TV on fourteen hours daily. It's our babysitter, our companion, teacher, big brother, and mom, putting us to sleep at night. There is no greater vehicle for propaganda. It influences and molds society's character and direction.

Compare the United States to elsewhere. Indisputably, we are the most violent society on earth. We have more people in prison, more murders, more suicides and more child abuse than any nation on this planet. Crime is rampant here, while in many other countries, the police don't even carry guns. Other countries don't show violence on TV, and consequently crime as an issue almost doesn't exist. There is virtually no street crime in Japan, Russia, China, and most of the Arab countries, and many others. Why are you safe in their streets at night, and why will no-one feel secure walking to their cars in the parking lot tonight?

Another trend that concerns me is the random violence directed at women. The movies most in demand because at a certain budget they're risk-free are what we call "slice and dice," and what you call Horror. Whether it's "Creepshow", or "Nightmare on Elm Street," or whatever else is opening this weekend, the victims are invariably young women. Would a social scientist call this a reaction to Women's Lib, or is it because men control the industry? Or is life imitating art?

We are what we consume, and as a consumer, you can make a choice as to what tickets you buy, or what shows you watch. You can make a difference, because life is not like it's portrayed in TV and films. And those of you who are studying the New Physics know that the observed changes with the observer - that all events everywhere in the universe are linked- that cause has effect, and that the Law of Attraction demands that violence attracts violence, and also that love attracts love.

You may have heard of the ancient Chinese curse "May you live in interesting times". Well, these are interesting times. We stand at a crossroads. The next 25 years are crucial for all of us. I suggest that we had better, and I mean all of us, take an especially close look at power in the media. And my hope is that those of you who enter this business use that power to help turn us around... to celebrating love and compassion, instead of what we're seeing today. Thank you."

Movies today, and cable TV, show everything. I mean, everything. From actors sitting on the toilet, to female and male frontal nudity, and sex practices that I would have paid all my allowance to see when I was 13. I read that PG-13 films today have three times more gun violence than films of the 1980s. And as for violence, has anyone seen *"Vikings"* on the History Channel?

And let's not leave out the kids: According to Ian Colman, PhD, of the University of Ottawa in Canada, and colleagues, analysis shows that kids' animated movies are rife with mayhem and murder. Wile E. Coyote spent 48 short subjects being variously impaled, crushed, pushed off cliffs, blown up, and otherwise afflicted with gross bodily harm to gleeful laughter from his youthful audience. And he's not the only one ... think of Daffy Duck. Yosemite Sam. Poor old Elmer "Shhhh, We're Hunting Wabbits" , said Elmer Fudd.

Violence was a way of death on the big screen back in the day. But that's just old cartoons, right? Nowadays, the big-budget animated movies -- *"Frozen,"* for instance, or *"Finding Nemo"* -- must be kinder and gentler, less ... well, violent. Not so, according to new research that suggests the cartoon mayhem of old extends to the long-form animated children's movie. In fact, if you're a main character in a kids' animated movie, you're more than twice as likely to die onscreen than your counterparts in an adult film. Characters are more likely to be murdered in the kids' flicks, compared with movies aimed at an adult audience. "When we started the study," Colman told *MedPage Today*, "we thought: Wouldn't it be funny if there were as many deaths in children's films as there were in films for adults?"

"You can imagine our surprise when we found that the death rate isn't equal, it's actually much higher," he said.

Although the analysis started out as a "bit of fun," he said, it addresses a long-running debate over the issue of violence in material aimed at kids. "You can go back to the Brothers Grimm -- and just how grim some of those fairy tales were," Colman said. What's new here, he said, is the use of epidemiological methods to try to quantify the issue. Colman and colleagues looked at the 45 top-grossing children's animated films of all time and compared them with the two top-grossing adult films of the same year. Films were included if they were animated and rated for either a general audience or with parental guidance (G or PG) and movies whose characters were neither humans nor animals were excluded. Titles ranged from 1937's "Snow White" to last year's "Frozen." The primary endpoint was the time to first on-screen death an important character, using a Kaplan-Meier survival analysis with Cox regression to compare the children's and adult movies. The researchers defined an important character as the main character, a friend or family member of a main character, or the main villain.

Colman and colleagues also looked at two secondary factors -- whether the death was murder and whether death happened to a parent of the main character.

After adjusting for runtime (since kids' movies are usually shorter) and years since release, the risk of on-screen death of important characters was significantly higher in children's films than in the 90-comparator movies.

The risk was similar over time, they found, noting that the interaction between film type and years since it was released did not predict mortality. Murder was also most foul in children's movies, and again the risk over time was not different. Finally, there was some evidence -- although it did not reach significance -- to suggest that the "Bambi's Mom" effect plays a greater role in children's movies. The risk of parental death was higher than in adult films.

The study has implications for parents, Colman said. "Just because a film has a cute clown fish, or a princess, or a beautiful baby deer as the main character doesn't mean there won't be murder and mayhem," he said. "There's a horrific death scene in the first five minutes of 'Finding Nemo.'"

Carlos Saura, whom I met with Geraldine Chaplin, when I was representing her after she made her film debut in *"Doctor Zhivago,"* told me that as a director, the Europeans would rather audiences saw a naked breast being fondled, than see it cut off.

Men's Beauty Tips

A 'penis whitening' service where men have their groins blasted with a laser is a huge hit with men in Thailand. The Lelax Hospital in Bangkok, says they do three to four clients per day. More than 100 men a month have been the clinic in Thailand, which specializes in penis whitening procedure.

Bunthita Wattanasiri, a manager for the Skin and Laser department at Lelax Hospital told AFP, that many come from Thailand's LGBTQ community.

Whitening and bleaching treatments are particularly popular in Thailand, where skin-whitening ads have caused outrage and accusations of racism.

Laser bleaching of private areas is carried out by using a type of laser which damages or kills the cells that produce melanin - the pigment that gives skin its color. Popularity of bleaching private parts has been linked to several high-profile celebrities, such as Kourtney Kardashian, publicly admitting to having these procedures done. HB Health of Knightsbridge, a leading medical aesthetic clinic based in London, reported a 23 per cent in the number of people - men and women - asking for anal bleaching in 2017.

Scrotoplasty is also very popular. Yes, there is an operation that removes saggy skin of your scrotum. Consultant plastic surgeon Gerard Lambe, in Cheshire and spokesperson for the British Association of Aesthetic Plastic Surgeons, told MailOnline the genital surgery was on the rise. He said the main reason behind the procedure is to reverse the side effects of ageing. Both male and female sexual organs shrink with age and scrotums sag. Like every other muscle, gravity rules. Imagine how one's saggy scrotum can get caught in clothing.

And male pubic hair removal has become mainstream. A survey by Gillette showed that one in five men like to look like pre-pubescent teenagers, matching women who shave their pussys, too. In the Gillette survey, an overwhelming 92 percent of women said they preferred a guy who was neat and tidy down below.

Male movie stars like Daniel Craig shave their chests, most people know, so why are men shaving their balls? I have friends in the Adult Film business – porn. Male participants are mostly hairless, reducing their female partners having to call a halt to production to dig the pubic hair out of their teeth. The same goes for gay porn, as well.

And have you heard of Scrotox? Men are to have Botox injected into their scrotums. The treatment, which costs $2,800, decreases sweating and reduces wrinkles

Lee Kynaston, writing in the Telegraph, tried out the Remington ball shaver. Known as the *Delicates & Body Hair Trimmer*, he read the instructions first, which he recommends. "Use slow and even strokes for the best results," it says, and "For hair in around your delicates, lift your delicate parts to get a clear view of the area you are trimming." I'd stick to using what's described as the 'detail blade' rather than the main blade if you're planning on having children."

"Please! What man in his right mind would ever do this?" Lee points out that the removal of body hair, including pubic hair, is both big business and a trend, even if Remington can't quite bring themselves to use the word balls.

What was first popular in the gay community is now being adopted by straight men. When I recently asked a good friend whether he was a fan of it, he replied: "Oh, yes. I take it all off – there's nothing there. Nada. My girlfriend loves it." Surprisingly, it turned out that the girlfriend in question actually had more hair than he did. "She has a landing strip," he said proudly, having clearly won the battle of the bush. Pornography also shapes men's perceptions of grooming down below.

Mark Simpson, author of Metrosexy: a 21st Century Self-Love Story, says, "This helps to 'show' as much 'sex' as possible – which is, after, all what porn is for.

But there's another benefit from having a smooth sac, as I discovered when I interviewed British porn director Anna Span a few years ago. "Removing the hair makes a man's balls look bigger and more impressive because, optically, anything that's light tends to look larger," she told me, adding that from a partner's perspective they were preferable as there were no rogue hairs to act as dental floss.
"There's nothing worse than bristly balls."

The Good News

Circumcised men may soon be able to regrow their foreskin. That's good news, especially in these days of sex diseases. Especially in Africa, where AIDS still is a concern. Add to that Zika, and a host of other infections, like herpes and the human papilloma virus. Scientists have shown that smegma, the waxy substance that hides under the foreskin, can host microbes that provide entry into vaginas, and if you like that style, anus'. A sister of a friend of mine, and her husband, was a campaigner against circumcision. The guy was angry that his parents gave him no say. They call themselves 'intactivists' and say it led to insensitivity. You will permit me a joke here: Two five-years were side by side in a hospital. "What are you in for," asked one boy. "Circumcision," said the other. "I had that when I was just born. I couldn't walk for a year."

There actually are websites such as foreskin-restoration.net and circumstitions.com, which angry men complain that they have de-sensitivity in their penises and cannot enjoy sex. I never had that problem. I think these guys wouldn't enjoy sex whatever.

A U.S. company, Foregen says it will soon be able to regrow foreskin by creating an extra-cellular matrix, a 'skeleton' for tissue, which provides an attachment point for cells and makes human tissue 3D, and causes regeneration. This extra-cellular matrix is then seeded with the appropriate layer of cells, in this case, stem cells that will grow into foreskin. It is experimenting on animals before trials on humans.

Scientists have also been able to regrow functioning penises in rabbits, so who knows – maybe these guys will be able to fuck like bunnies when they have a foreskin once more.

Threesomes, Anyone?

A British sociologist reveals how straight men are increasingly having a ménage à trois with other males as a way to strengthen their bromances. Harry Pettit, writing in Mailonline, says Dr. Ryan Scoats, from Birmingham City University, specializes in threesomes. Imagine that, a PhD in threesomes! Women are often intimidated by the thought of a threesome with two men, but many men reported that these encounters are a way to bond with their closest male friends. Scoats said that the rise of the 'bromance' and decline in homophobia in western societies is helping to make MMF threesomes more acceptable.

Watching your wife have sex is GOOD for couples

The various porn sites have an entire audience segment devoted to fantasies of watching your spouse or significant other have sex with another – of any sexual persuasion, or in groups. I did the same in my pre-1981 swinging days, before AIDS appeared, in order to 'freeze' sexual behavior! I've always believed that nature tries in vain to limit human reproduction to save the other species, - animal, vegetable or mineral, from extinction – which unchecked growth of homo sapiens, will do. AIDS was, in my opinion, meant to limit humans from having babies, as Zika today is meant to do. Cancer, too. The flu epidemic of 1918, was the same, and wars, which kill millions of people, still rage, based on our animal instincts. But we humans, being clever and scientific, manage to outwit nature and still keep overpopulating the planet. One wonders what the next plague will be – and whether we'll avoid it.

Watching your partner have sex with another person can strengthen your relationship, some scientists say. Psychologist Dr David Ley, author of *'Insatiable Wives'''* and Dr Justin Lehmiller, a psychologist at Ball State University, report some people have 'cuckold fantasies' in which their partner cheats on them. They claim cuckolding couples who act on their desires feel liberated, and allows them to enjoy better communication skills than other couples. An article in CNN, says cuckoldry is increasingly becoming a popular and sought-out fetish. Research shows that 58 per cent of men and one in three women have fantasized about cuckolding.

Shockwaves For Sex

Megan Sheets, writing for Dailymail.com, says that Jason's doctor, urologist Paul Savage, founder and lead physician at the Agenix clinic in Chicago, introduced him to shockwave therapy, which uses sound vibrations to increase blood flow in the penis, which results in intense sex and stronger orgasms. Shockwave therapy, not yet FDA-approved, has been used for kidney stones and heart problems, and is called lithotripsy, but it wasn't until 2012 that the machine used to create the acoustic vibrations was tested on erectile dysfunction. Hundreds of clinics around the U.S now offer the treatment that uses sound waves to open small blood vessels in the penis, removing plaque build-up and allowing for more blood flow. It also encourages new blood vessel and stem cell growth that can restore function. Dr. Savage calls it GAINSwave, and uses a lubricated probe to the penis, which turns red, meaning it's working, and administers acoustic vibrations to different areas.

Safe sex

Some people say there is no such thing. But in some cases, consensual nonmonogamy may be the choice. The University of Michigan's has found that people who cheat on their partners sexually are less likely to engage in safe sex while doing so than are people in consensual nonmonogamous relationships. The findings, published in March 2012 in the *Journal of Sexual Medicine*, apply to condom use, use of gloves for genital touching, discussion of sexually transmitted disease and sexual history and sterilization of sex toys. Sounds like NO fun.

Part of the reason for the difference may be that consensually nonmonogamous people often require that outside sex is okay, as long as it is safe. Cheaters were also more likely than consensually nonmonogamous people to be drunk or on drugs during their outside encounters. Nonexclusive hook-up culture has millenniums negotiating consensual nonmonogamy.

We Can't Afford Sex

My doctor, Gene Fishman, suggested canadiandrugs.com for me to be able to afford Viagra or Cialis. Drugs prices are out of control. One of life's great pleasures — sex, is now too expensive. Viagra and Cialis cost about $50 a pill, triple their 2010 list prices, according to Truven Health Analytics data. The new 'female Viagra,' a pill called Addyi, costs $800 per month. Women I know say it doesn't work.

The Associated Press say patients have told them they've given up sex because of the cost. Generic Viagra is now available, but still costs the same, a mystery to me. How does the manufacturer, Pfizer, expect to sell generic Viagra at much the same price as the now-off patent original? Divorced or widowed men and women are looking for sex partners. Drug prices in the U.S. are not regulated, whereas some countries, mostly with health plans for *all* citizens, exist.

The Sex Addiction Epidemic

Sex is a form of self-medication - to deal with anxiety, despair, and fear of emotional intimacy. "Sex addiction" is usually said to be a myth despite accounts by high-profile guys like Tiger Woods, Michael Douglas – and me! Compulsive sexual behavior wrecks marriages, in my case, two. Destroys careers, me, again. Americans are being diagnosed as sex -addicts in massive numbers. It destroys a person's life much as addictions to alcohol or drugs can.

The Society for the Advancement of Sexual Health, an education and sex-addiction treatment organization, estimates that between 3 and 5 percent of the U.S. population—or more than 9 million people—could meet the criteria for addiction. Some 1,500 sex therapists treating compulsive behavior are practicing today, up from fewer than 100 a decade ago, a jolly good increase. A lot of these are just jumping on the bandwagon, going where the money is, while the money's there.

Demographics now include women, teenagers and elderly folks. It's the reason why there are so many porn sites on the Internet. 40 million people a day in the U.S. log on to some 4.2 million pornographic websites, according to the Internet Filter Software Review.

And technology also facilitates hookups via the Smartphone in your pocket, and apps like Grindr that use GPS technology to gay hookups in 192 countries. AshleyMadison.com, which says it has 12.2 million members, connects people looking for sex outside their marriages. The Logo television network is broadcasting *Bad Sex*, a reality series following men and women with sex addiction. The movie *Shame* might have been about me. I even joined a Sex and Love Addicts Anonymous 12-step program. Director and co-writer, Steve McQueen says, "What we were doing was actually psychologically dangerous."

Treatment programs are modeled on Alcoholics Anonymous, which is the only system, in my opinion, that works. The aim is for "sexual sobriety." Sex addiction is obsessive-compulsive disorder. Sex addicts are driven by the same emotional cues that drive alcoholics, or gambling, or food, or drug addicts. Dopamine, the brain's mood regulator is addictive in itself, and getting the dopamine high is what sex addicts crave. 90 percent of sex addicts are men. But 10 percent are women– and there are lots of them. Women are "love addicts," with a tendency for dependent relationships. Everybody knows someone who refuses to leave a marriage or relationship no matter the beatings they take, emotional or physically.

Sex Addiction is one step closer to becoming a recognized disorder, says Dennis Romero in the LA Weekly. UCLA has come up with a set of scientific criteria for sex addiction. And the new guidelines make this one step closer to becoming recognized as a legitimate mental disorder along the lines of drug addiction.

Published in the latest *Journal of Sexual Medicine*, the new guidelines will allow the editors of upcoming, fifth edition of psychiatry's bible, the *Diagnostic and Statistical Manual of Mental Disorders* to seriously consider induction of sex addiction as a real condition. Rory Reid, assistant professor of psychiatry at the Semel Institute of Neuroscience and Human Behavior at UCLA, says that one indication is a recurring pattern of sexual fantasies, urges and behaviors lasting a period of six months or longer that are not caused by other issues, such as substance abuse, another medical condition or manic episodes associated with bipolar disorder. Another is a pattern of sexual activity in response to unpleasant mood states, such as feeling depressed, or a pattern of repeatedly using sex as a way of coping with stress, or unsuccessful attempts to reduce or stop sexual activities that are problematic.

The Third Sex

I was one of the judges in the 2009 Miss Thailand Pageant. I was doing business in Thailand, and my hosts gave a party benefiting the Princess's charities at the Mandarin Hotel, to which the cream of Thai society - politicians, military officers, and top businessmen and their wives were invited. It was the occasion of the publication of my biography, *"All is Vanity,"* and a gala affair it is was. A copy of my book, signed by me, was auctioned off for $5,000 US dollars to benefit the Princess' fund.

The big story about the previous Miss Thailand Pageant was that a third sex person won it. Third sex is a recognized sex in Thailand, positioned after the usual male-female duo. One of the government ministers I met at the party was a third sex person. Thailand is known as a getaway for plastic surgery. Physical enhancement is very big in Thailand – the prices are low, compared to other places, chiefly the U.S., doctors are expert and accommodations first class. Many of the women I met in Bangkok were originally men, or boys. They were among the most beautiful people I ever saw, and considering I was deeply involved in beautiful women as an publicist, theatrical agent and producer in Hollywood, that is saying something. My hosts made sure I was well provisioned while I was in Bangkok. I've always wondered if….

That year, their DNA certified the contestants were all female.

As reported by Flora Drury For Mailonline, published January 2016, sequins, spangles and tiaras: The beauty pageant full of gorgeous women with a shocking surprise – they were all born men. The women lined up on stage are some of the most beautiful you will ever see. Miss Tiffany Universe, Thailand, is world's most popular transgender pageant where all entries used to be male. Every year, 100 wear heavy make up, do their hair and don tight-fitting sequin dresses to win the beauty contest. Typical of other pageants, the women all battle it out and shimmy along the stage in swimsuit and ball gown rounds. The winner is awarded a year's salary in Thailand, a car - and acceptance from the wider community.

Women's Sex Beauty Tips

Every now and then I imagine myself as female – usually during sex. To receive – not to give – to be the recipient – to work less hard, not to raise a sweat. Not to worry about getting an erection and not performing. Then I say, with all the hardships of being a male, "fuck it, I'm glad to be a man."

Women have to labor hard to be attractive to men – or women – as they get older. The cosmetics business is a billion dollar a year industry. As I said previously, I owned a cosmetics company. As I got to know the industry, I found that it was basically a scam – LaPrairie grinds up a little seaweed and calls it "from the sea," or something like that, and adds a few fish eggs and calls its line "Caviar." All brands are basically the same – lanolin, from sheep, and trace elements added, in order to cajole women – and men – into paying hundreds of dollars for the same ingredients as baby cream.

There are weird ingredients added to cosmetics, which are endorsed by "skin gurus," or are endorsed by celebrities in exchange for large cash outlays, or shares in a public company. Some of those "ingredients are baby foreskin, semen, placenta, and bird poop. Several skincare products are made with placenta, including an $850 cream by Rodial. HydraFacial MD uses baby foreskin in its treatment, harvesting about a million stem cells from a single piece of skin.

I've heard jokes about using foreskin as wallets, just rub it a few times and it grows into a suitcase.

Snail slime has been pioneered by Korean companies and is supposed to hydrate skin and increase suppleness.

Celebrities get facials featuring 'uguisu, which literally translates to nightingale feces. Bird poop was said to have been first used in skin treatments in 17th century Japan, when geisha found that it repaired skin damaged by the lead-based make-up they wore. I said before that Tom Cruise says it's what keeps him looking so young.

Heather Locklear admitted in 2013 that she rubs semen on her face for better skin. UK beauty vlogger Tracy Kiss swore by this treatment, insisting that rubbing semen donated by a male friend all over her face was the key to her complexion. 'It feels so glossy to wipe it off. It feels like having a kind of oil on the face,' she explained. 'It just glides beautifully.'

Sheep sebum is also called lanolin - oil made from sheep skin.

Marijuana is in the news today. I use it. CBD is the non-psychoactive version. I had a minor operation by my dermatologist at UCLA, in which he sliced off some skin from my ear and sent it for biopsy – the sun is poison, and when you live in Los Angeles, where the sun is your companion for 345 days a year, skin cancer is your other companion. My ear wouldn't heal – he said it would, but it wouldn't. Until I started using Hemp Oil – that's what the government allows manufactures to call it. In less than a week, there was no trace of the wound. I'm using it on my face. My girlfriend says I look younger.

Gwyneth Paltrow advised her readers of the importance of getting V-Steams — a spa treatment that cleanses a customer's vaginas'. Available on Paltrow's website are 'eggs' made out of semi-precious stones, to be inserted in a woman's vagina in order to improve one's kegel responses and to increase orgasms.

Writing about a high-end Santa Monica retreat called Tikkun Holistic Spa, Paltrow says, "The real golden ticket here is the Mugworth V-Steam: You sit on what is essentially a mini-throne, and a combination of infrared and mugwort steam cleanses your uterus, et al." Us Weekly says that Paltrow practices what she preaches. "It is an energetic release — not just a steam douche — that balances female hormone levels," she adds. "If you're in L.A., you have to do it."

Have a 'bad belly button?"

Belly buttons are the new plastic surgery craze. Surgeon reports huge surge in patients wanting a 'hooded oval' like Emily Ratajkowski. Interest in belly button revisions, called umbilicoplasty has doubled in recent years, and they attribute this to camera phones and social media sites like Instagram. Jaleesa Baulkman For Dailymail.com, reports that Americans have spent about $16 billion on cosmetic plastic surgery in 2016.

Dr. Matthew Schulman, a board-certified plastic surgeon, said people are more likely to do something about their belly buttons right before the spring or summer season, and the number of belly button revisions he's performed has doubled over the past five and six years. 'The belly button is an important part of your anatomy from a cosmetic perspective,' Dr Thomas Sperry, another board-certified plastic surgeon, said, 'If you're at the beach ... and you got a bad belly button, it's hard to look sexy,' Dr Sperry added. Dr Schulman said the ideal belly button is an oval that's vertically oriented because it makes the torso look longer and the abs leaner. 'When it comes to belly buttons people would more often bring Victoria Secret catalogs,' he said. Meanwhile, many of Dr Schulman's patients have requested an innie belly button - a conclave navel - that's slightly hooded.

Dr David Shafer, still another board certified plastic surgeon and RealSelf contributor, said that many patients come in to get their belly button piercing removed. 'All those people who got their belly buttons pierced in the 90s are now around 35 and their piercing looks funny' due to weight gain or pregnancy.

Uh, Oh

Trend Micro spokesman, Udo Schneider, surprised journalists at a news conference by placing a large, neon-pink vibrator on the desk in front of him and then bringing it to life by typing out a few lines of code on his laptop. While the stunt provoked giggles, the message was sobering. As the number of smart, interactive devices connected to the Internet explodes, concern is mounting about insufficient safeguards and a lack of consumer and employee awareness. So you butt plug fanciers, beware.

The Vagina Whisperer

Plastic surgeon Dr Amir Marashi, known as the 'vagina whisperer', has performed over 400 vaginoplasties, reports Mary Kekatos for Dailymail.com. He is New York's star surgeon, who spends every minute of every day designing perfect vaginas for women. Sounds like a dream job. Latest figures show over 5,000 women receive the surgery in the US each year. The rise is particularly in younger women as they see celebrities show off their 'designer vaginas'. There are two reasons women come in - the first is cosmetic; women feel uncomfortable about the size, the shape, or even color of their vagina. The surgeon can shorten the labia, lighten the color, make the vagina moister, and amplify the G-spot.

Procedures include Labiaplasty - shortening or reshaping the vaginal lips, tightening the vagina, Clitoridotomy - reducing the clitoral hood, Hymenoplasty - reconstruction of the hymen, especially good if you want to be a virgin once again. Celebrities showing off their 'designer vaginas' include British model Katie Price and Real Housewives of Beverly Hills star, Brandi Glanville.

Another surgeon says the sharp rise in 'designer vagina' surgery is a desire 'to look good in yoga pants and bikinis'. Dr Jennifer Walden, an aesthetic plastic surgeon says Labiaplasty is the 'most popular cosmetic op for women'. Women are more aware of their genital area because of access to porn on the Internet, and the trend for total pubic hair removal.

And teenage girls are nagging their doctors about getting their labia shaped. The American College of Obstetricians and Gynecologists (ACOG) has issued guidelines on how doctors should talk with adolescents about labiaplasty, a surgical reduction of the labia that is often done for cosmetic reasons. "Variety in the shape, size, appearance and symmetry of labia can have particularly distressing psychological effects on young women," said Julie Strickland, the chair of ACOG's Adolescent Health Care Committee and lead author of the paper, in a press release. "It's one more body part that women are insecure about and it's our job, as ob-gyns, to reassure our young patients." This matters because, as Strickland put it to Vocativ, "labiaplasty is not a minor procedure"—and it comes with the risk of serious complications, including pain, scarring and infection.

The number of girls age 18 and under obtaining labiaplasties in the United States has nearly doubled, according to the American Society of Aesthetic Plastic Surgery.

The ACOG paper says, "Increasing trends in pubic hair removal, exposure to idealized images of genital anatomy, and increasing awareness of cosmetic vaginal surgery have been proposed as reasons for the increased interest in labial surgery." In other words, waxing, porn and advertising.

Besides Mae West's daily enema, which she swore was what kept her skin so beautiful until she died, Preparation H, applied generously to the skin at bedtime, is what many Hollywood actresses use to keep the wrinkles at bay. Yeah, the very same Preparation H sold in drugstores meant to reduce hemorrhoids. Try it, you'll like it.

And in Beverly Hills, you can get a Butt Facial. No kidding, in fact BH is known as the *home* of the famous Butt Facial.

Speaking of Vaginas

Jessica Rach For Mailonline reports that a new mother had her placenta turned into a batch of chocolates - and documented the entire process on Snapchat. Beautician Kiley Witworth, 23, from Georgia, who gave birth to son Samuel, hired a professional to whip up a batch of the chocolates - which she claims will improve her postnatal health - after spotting a business card for placenta encapsulation on the maternity ward. She then filmed the organ being dehydrated, blended and turned into truffles and heart-shaped chocolates on her Snapchat - complete with footage of her sampling them the treats for the first time. The footage has divided viewers, with some branding it 'cannibalism', while others applaud Kiley's choice.

The Answer

Maybe the answer for future relationships that have sex as their basis, including Hollywood, is an App. A new app clears up the issue of consent between sexual partners, by creating legally binding contracts. The software hopes to help protect against STDs and 'revenge porn', as well as making clear what each person is comfortable with in the bedroom. Agreements made via the app, which will be available on iOS and Android, can be accepted with a tap of a smartphone's screen.

The app generates a Live Contract, which is a legally binding agreement. Live Contract is only shared between the parties involved, and is placed in the blockchain, a continuously growing list of records, called blocks, which are linked and secured using encryption. Users can change their mind at any time and being passed out means no at any time, according to the terms of the agreement. You can withdraw consent through the LegalFling app with a single tap. If a breach of contract does occur, the app claims users can trigger 'cease and desist' letters and enforcing penalty payments,' as well as make it easier to bring the case to court.

LegalFling, by Dutch firm LegalThings, is designed to ensure that explicit consent is given before participants engage in sexual behavior.

As well as sending your request for consensual sex to your contact of choice, the app also lets you set your sexual preferences, including your list of do's and don'ts.

That includes options such as approval for photos and videos to be made, whether a condom should be used, a guarantee that prospective partners are STD-free and whether you are comfortable with the use of explicit language and BDSM.

While it may be of use for one-night stands, its creators believe it could help to protect many different kinds of sexual activity, including in long-term relationships. 'While you're protected by law, litigating any offenses through court is nearly impossible in reality'.

The Bad News

As if men needed another thing to be scared of in the bedroom. Scientists at University of Mississippi have warned that erectile dysfunction increases the risk of early death by 70%, because it is an important marker of cardiovascular risk. Erectile dysfunction most often affects older men, but nearly 20 per cent of men under the age of 40 are targeted by it, researchers said. Hyperlipidemia, hypertension, obesity, diabetes and smoking can also contribute.

More bad news for men is that men who have "playboy" attitudes and believe in power over women may face a higher risk for mental health trouble than men who don't, a broad new research review suggests. The finding on sexism, and other so-called "traditional views" on masculinity, stems from an analysis of 74 studies conducted between 2003 and 2013. The studies included nearly 19,500 predominantly white male participants, the researchers said. Study lead author Y. Joel Wong, remarked, "What we found overall is that the more that men conformed to masculine norms the poorer their mental health, and the less likely they were to seek mental health services," he said. Wong is associate professor of counseling and educational psychology at Indiana University Bloomington. Wong's team published the findings in the Nov. 21, 2017 online issue of the *Journal of Counseling Psychology*.

Even More Bad News

The end of men? Experts tell how the male sex chromosome could one day disappear completely. University of Kent researchers have found the Y chromosome is shrinking. The Y chromosome plays a critical role in the sexual reproduction of men. The male sex chromosome determines the biological sex of an unborn baby. It has been shrinking over generations and is expected to go extinct in less than five million years – if we are around by then – which I doubt.

In an article for The Conversation, Dr Peter Ellis and professor Darren Griffin from the University of Kent discuss the implications of this genetic shift. The number of genes on the Y has dropped from over 1,000 to roughly 50, a loss of more than 95 per cent.

Japanese spiny rats and mole voles have lost their Y-chromosomes entirely – and the processes of genes being lost or created on the Y-chromosome could see the formation of entirely new species. This means that genetic engineering may soon be able to replace the gene function of the Y chromosome, allowing same-sex female couples or infertile men to conceive.

Polyamory

In the 1970s, as I wrote in my book, *"All is Vanity,"* partner swapping and swinging was very popular. This coincided with the female 'birth control" pill, so that pregnancy was no longer a concomitant. That came to a full stop in 1981, when AIDS was an issue. Now that it's controlled, and the genus of AIDS has been found to be manageable, we're not scared of it anymore. However, some older folks are still worried about it, and their doctors warn seniors just to say 'no.'

But people love sex, which takes their minds off what is happening at home, or in Washington, D.C., or the world. I know folks who still 'swing,' and I know some people who are in love, or lust, with several others.

University of Michigan psychologist Terri Conley has estimated that about 5 percent of Americans are in one of these types of relationships. Scientists know lesbian, gay and bisexual individuals are more likely than heterosexuals to enter nonmonogamous relationships. Those types are more open to new experiences. An estimated 4 to 5 percent of Americans are looking outside their relationship for love and sex — with their partner's full permission.

Consensually nonmonogamous relationships don't conform to anything that's 'accepted' by society, from "swinging" and open relationships to long-term commitments among multiple people. Psychologists say they may even change monogamy for the better. "People in these relationships really communicate. They communicate to death," said Bjarne Holmes, a psychologist at Champlain College in Vermont. All of that negotiation may hold a lesson for the monogamously inclined, Holmes told LiveScience. "They are potentially doing quite a lot of things that could turn out to be things that if people who are practicing monogamy did more of, their relationships would actually be better off," Holmes said.

There's a joke concerning Donald Trump – He's in an elevator going up in his Trump Tower, when it stops on a floor, and a beautiful girl enters, sees it's him, and exclaims, "Donald Trump! I've dreamed of this moment. I want to suck your cock and fuck you to death." He thinks about it for a moment, and then says, "Ok, but what's in it for me?"

"I myself am heaven and hell"
Omar Khayyam (Rubaiyat)